Leading Small Groups
Basic Skills for Church and Community Organizations

Nathan W. Turner

Judson Press ® Valley Forge

Leading Small Groups: Basic Skills for Church and Community Organizations
© 1996 Judson Press, Valley Forge, PA 19482-0851

Library of Congress Cataloging-in-Publication Data
Turner, Nathan W.
  Leading small groups : basic skills for church and community organizations /
Nathan W. Turner.
    p. cm.
  Includes bibliographical references.
  ISBN 0-8170-1210-9 (pbk. : alk. paper)
  1. Church group work. 2. Christian leadership. I. Title.
BV652.2 T87 1996
253'.7—dc20   96-35575

Printed in the U.S.A.
05 04 03 02 01 00 99 98 97
10 9 8 7 6 5 4 3 2 1

To Marj,
who has expanded my knowledge
of small groups by
her perceptive observations
and sage questions

Contents

Acknowledgments

I would like to acknowledge numerous persons whose influence on me over the years is reflected in some of my insights and statements. Although I assume full responsibility for the content of the book, it is with a spirit of appreciation that I acknowledge those who have been positive and challenging influences on my insights into small groups.

A special word of appreciation goes to Kristy Pullen of Judson Press, without whose words of encouragement and technical assistance this book might not have been written. I am also grateful for the helpful work of Victoria McGoey and Mary Nicol, also at Judson. Additional apppreciation is extended to Donna Fackler, Doug Congdon-Martin, Lisa and Phil Mugridge, and Steve and Dave Turner for technical computer assistance.

For some of the small-group charts and concepts in parts of this book, I want to express my appreciation for the work of Miriam A. Peterson in her earlier small-group monographs, published years ago.

For these persons, and countless others, I wish to express a word of personal gratitude.

Introduction

This book is intended as an introductory text for leaders, facilitators, and teachers of small groups within religious, voluntary, community, and other social organizations. Leaders of such groups have wanted to be effective in their small-group leadership; consequently, this book is specifically focused on their leadership needs. Its brief chapters will guide the reader through general background information about small groups to more specific "how to" types of information. Training-workshop outlines and a special resource section will conclude this revised edition of the earlier book entitled *Effective Leadership in Small Groups*.

Leaders of small groups can enable a group to identify what has been happening in the group in a number of ways:

1. The group leader can learn to trust his or her own feelings, hunches, and intuition and to share such feelings with the group.

2. The group leader can assist the group in analyzing its own behavior and in discovering what is happening within the group. A way to do such discovering is to invite feedback from the group in order to test out feelings and ideas.

3. The group leader can lead the group in analyzing the verbal content of what goes on, the particular stage of group development, the decision-making process and its effective functioning, and the degree of personal interest and involvement each member has in what has been happening.

4. The leader can ask for a discussion about what has not been happening and how the group feels about omissions and/or lack of progress. It is often wise to secure suggestions from members about

how to change so that progress can be made.

You will find numerous uses for this book. It may be used as a basic text and guidebook for leaders, facilitators, teachers, and group leaders. Teachers and leaders of youth and adult classes or groups may find it a valuable guide to keep handy. Workshop, seminar, and program leaders will also find it helpful. Chapter 7, "Training Workshops for Small-Group Leaders," is designed to be used by a church, community, or voluntary group to train teachers, board and committee leaders, and small-group facilitators. Professional group leaders desiring a brief book on small-group facilitation and leadership will find it a basic resource. A significant section of resources has been added that includes charts and valuable information on a variety of topics, all of which will provide handouts for small-group leaders to use. Finally, anyone interested in the dynamics of small groups will find this book helpful.

Chapter 1

Basic Leadership Skills

In order to lead a small group effectively, one needs to know something about the *context* of the group, the *norms and processes,* what goes into being a *group facilitator* or *leader,* and the difference between *task and maintenance roles* that members provide. The purpose of this first chapter is to discuss these four areas.

Contexts of Groups

The context in which a group exists can influence its functions, its expectations, and the type of leadership it requires. Group contexts include the church, the home, camp and conference centers, community organizations, and other voluntary groups. Obviously there are many more contexts in which groups function, and this list is only suggestive.

Within a given context, both group leaders and group members may make assumptions about the group. When such assumptions are made, personal expectations are formed by each individual. Too often these are not shared or checked. When these assumptions and expectations begin to operate within the group process, confusion, misunderstandings, and conflict may arise unnecessarily. For example, say the group context is a community group. If a participant expects a lot of structure and organization, he or she can be frustrated and disappointed if the leader provides only minimal organization.

The *context* of a group includes the physical environment. The color of the room, the furnishings, the total decor, plus the color of the clothing of the group members all have an impact on the group's context. Furthermore, the time of day, the day of the week, the noise level, and the weather can influence the group and the members' responses to one another.

An additional context for a group is its psychological or emotional composition. For example, if the group comes into the room anticipating trouble, the group will likely find the trouble it was fearing. If a group enters a room anticipating a positive and productive session, it will likely experience much of what was anticipated. Some psychologists say that we experience what we prophesy will happen; this process is often termed a "self-fulfilling prophecy." Self-fulfilling prophecies can and do become part of the overall group context that influences how a group functions.

Organizational Context of Groups

The context for a small group is often influenced by the culture of the parent organization, which upholds the values and beliefs that guide its behavior. Yet it is possible for a small group to hold or develop a "group culture" that differs from the larger organizational culture of which it is a member. For effectiveness, it is important for the organizational culture to be supportive of its small groups and vice versa.

Organizational context generally includes (1) a clear mission statement and a shared meaning and vision, (2) a supportive culture, (3) shared information open to all, (4) a feedback system, (5) a reward/recognition system, (6) a training system for leaders and group members, (7) necessary resources, and (8) an appropriate physical environment.

Group Norms

Groups typically have norms by which they are known.[1] Some group members tend to remain silent, thereby permitting a majority of highly verbal ones to do all the talking. Other groups may have members who are very reluctant to talk, with only a few members who participate verbally. A norm for certain groups is formality, including the use of titles, taking action according to Robert's Rules of Order, and recording everything in the minutes.

Some group norms are known and articulated. Other norms are unarticulated and invisible but still operative. When a new member unknowingly crosses an invisible line, that member may be admonished for breaking a group norm he or she had no way of knowing about. The attitude is "you were supposed to know!" A common example is when a new group member speaks up and is admonished for speaking. It is only then that the new group member "discovers" the invisible norm which says that "new members are to be silent and observe, but are not to participate verbally until we tell them. In the meantime, we will not tell them; just let them find it out on their own."

Effective Group Norms

Every member has a responsibility to help the group develop norms and functions that assist the group to be productive. An effective group will develop and operate on some or all of the following norms or standards:

1. *Acceptance.* Persons are accepting of other members rather than rejecting.

2. *Freedom of Expression.* Persons feel free to express their ideas and feelings honestly and openly during times of agreement and disagreement.

3. *Member Participation.* All members are encouraged to participate so as to feel included and to foster maximum exchange of ideas, information, and options.

4. *Listening.* Persons actively listen to each one who speaks by indicating that the person is understood and by asking questions that elicit more information when desired.

5. *Dealing with Feelings.* Even in task groups, times occur when personal feelings need to be dealt with and resolved before further progress can be made.

6. *Dealing with Differences.* The expression of differences is normal and inevitable in groups of people. Realizing that differences can stretch thinking and eventually lead to better group decisions and solutions, it is crucial that effective leaders of small

groups learn conflict management skills that enable them to deal with differences. The repression, denial, or avoidance of differences leads only to more serious conflicts in the future. Power struggles, control issues, and turf battles signal deeper differences needing discussion and resolution.

7. *Commitment to the Group's Purpose.* Small groups usually have a stated purpose and set of goals. It is normative to expect group members to support and carry out the group's purpose and goals. However, if a person joins a group only for social reasons and has, for example, only a 10 percent commitment to the group's purposes while others display a 90- to 100-percent commitment, differences will occur! At times it is important to verbally test for commitment to a group's purpose and goals before proceeding. It is commonplace in religious and voluntary organizations for at least a few persons to join primarily for social reasons. They are not 100 percent committed to the group or parent organization's purposes. People seldom want to discuss this in such organizations, yet this dynamic can exist and inadvertently block or slow down a group's progress.

8. *Openly Dealing with the Group Process.* Most small groups deal only with the *content* of the task or content on which the group is working. *Process* is how a group works together, including how members talk, relate, agree or disagree, make decisions, solve problems, and nonverbally work with one another.

9. *Attendance.* When even one person arrives late or leaves early, it has a significant impact on the group's functioning. It is crucial that all be present for the total time agreed upon. Irregular attendance also has a negative impact on the group's development and functioning. In brief, everyone is important and needs to be present during the total time agreed to. A visitor to a group also has an impact on its functioning. The usual impact is that the group automatically regresses to an earlier stage of development. (See chapter two for more information on group stages.)

10. *Leadership.* One of the most common group norms is that it is the *leader's responsibility to keep the group moving and on track.* However, some small groups set a different norm requiring that all group members share the responsibility to keep things moving and

to share equally in dealing with the total group process. Hence, all group members share in the leadership functioning of the group in addition to the official leader.

11. *Changing Norms.* Some groups simply agree to review their operational norms periodically and to be flexible in changing norms as needed for the optimal functioning of their group.

Ineffective Group Norms

1. *Hidden Agendas.* Hidden agendas represent all the individual and/or group issues that differ from the surface agendas. Hidden agendas can be conscious or unconscious, known or unknown, felt or unfelt, apparent or unapparent. They can get in the way of the surface agendas or even block them from moving forward for any group progress and achievement. Common hidden agendas include special interests, ego, control, divided loyalties, insecurity, desires for the group to work on something else, competition with others in the group, resentment towards the group leader or parent organization, or lack of commitment to the group's public agenda and stated purpose.

2. *Secrets and Confidentiality.* One of the most destructive dynamics in small groups and organization is when some members agree to keep something secret or confidential. Few things need to be kept secret or confidential. The negative impact on a group is serious when members discover that important information or data was withheld by either their official leader or other group members. In such a case, a breach of trust and confidence has occurred, and once trust is violated, it takes a long time to rebuild it. Yet, if a small group has a known but unarticulated norm that is is acceptable to keep secrets from one another, how can they ever build trust in the group? On what level do they believe one another? Research tends to show that most secrets or confidential information is shared with at least one other person within one or two days' time. What does this say to us about the ability of human nature to hold on to such information? It is important to consider what this means for the development of a small group or a total organization.

Factors That Affect a Group

Certain factors are important for effective group functioning:

1. *Limit the Size.* For effective discussion, the size of the group needs to be kept at ten to twelve persons. An ideal group size for discussion is about five to seven persons, depending on the purpose to be achieved. If larger numbers are involved, then subdivide into groups of ten or fewer for the best discussion. Subgroups need not report back verbally unless the data will be used immediately. Subgroups may be asked to keep written notes to turn in later for compiling the group's overall thoughts, conclusions, or recommendations for the parent organization. When a group is fewer than five members, it may not contain within itself sufficient personal experiences or resources to produce meaningful dialogue or effective decisions. When a group becomes too large, it is impossible for all of its members to participate meaningfully, and usually the more verbally assertive ones tend to dominate and control the discussion. The following diagrams indicate the number of interpersonal relationships in groups of varying sizes and how quickly a geometric leap occurs in the number of relationships that potentially occur by adding another few persons:[2]

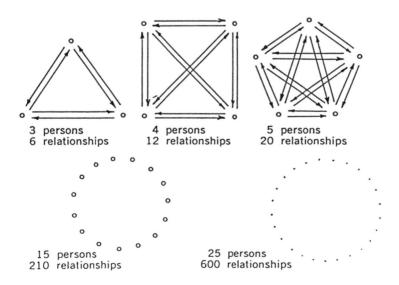

3 persons
6 relationships

4 persons
12 relationships

5 persons
20 relationships

15 persons
210 relationships

25 persons
600 relationships

2. *Make a Contract.* Persons need to agree to why they are meeting (purpose), for how long, who is to lead and record actions, who will carry out the decisions (delegate responsibility), and who will evaluate the process.

3. *Clarify Roles.* It is valuable to a group if the members clarify the roles of the leader(s) and group members and/or anyone else present so that everyone is clear about what to expect from one another. The processes involved in a group are complex and often function silently rather than verbally. Symptoms signaling that something is amiss in the group include apathy, anger, boredom, impersonal comments, conflict avoidance, gross confusion, constantly asking to clarify the goals because they are unclear, persons vying for leadership, sexist and racial/ethnic jokes and derogatory comments, and inappropriate humor (that is, jokes at a serious time). When such symptoms appear, they are a message to the group leader that something within the group needs attention.

These symptoms invite the leader to become active by asking the group if something needs attention and helping them identify the problem. The remaining chapters in this book will provide guidelines for the leader on how to deal with such symptoms in a group.

Desirable Group Characteristics

A group that functions effectively has certain desirable characteristics for which each member should assume responsibility. They include:

1. *Group Acceptance.* Each member accepts every other member as a person of worth, leaving no one feeling rejected or not desired in that group.

2. *Discussion Norms.* Members learn to understand the feelings of others and show respect for others, whether they agree with them or not.

3. *Learning to Listen.* Group members learn to listen to one another so they all feel an equal opportunity to participate. Each person is listened to and asked questions until the others can say they understand what the other person says as well as what they

mean by their statements. Usually we are in too much of a rush to take the time to really listen to one another.

4. *Freedom of Expression.* Members are encouraged to freely participate and welcome a diversity of opinions, including a minority position that differs from the majority viewpoint.

5. *Maximum Participation.* Conversation flows back and forth among group members so that ideas and opinions may be freely communicated and heard.

6. *Openness to Differences.* A group needs to be open to differences of all kinds if it expects to develop and work on an optimal level of productivity and effectiveness. Suppressing any conflicts or differences in ideas or opinions will predetermine a group to achieve its lowest level of development and accomplishment.

Roles of a Leader

To be an effective leader of a small group, one needs to develop and use a broad series of different leader behaviors and roles. Most of us tend to overuse one, two, or three behaviors in leading a small group. The challenge is to develop and practice a wider scope of effective leadership behaviors such as the following typical behaviors (shown below on a sliding scale of one to ten). That is, the leader would be as comfortable talking or listening, depending on which end of the sliding scale that behavior seemed appropriate to help facilitate the group discussion or decision making:

```
talking . . . . . . . . . . . . . . . . . . . . listening
questioning . . . . . . . . . . . . . . . . . . stating
dominating . . . . . . . . . . . . . . . . . .submitting
telling . . . . . . . . . . . . . . . . . . . . selling
consensus . . . . . . . . . . . . . . . . . . . voting
utilizing conflict . . . . . . . . . . . . . . avoiding it
1    . . . . . . . . . . . . 5 . . . . . . . . . . . . . 10
```

It is important to envision oneself as a leader with a wide range of skills on a one to ten scale. An effective leader will have some ability to use a range of leadership skills ranging from one to ten.

The Group Facilitator

One of the most helpful books I have read in recent years is *The Skilled Facilitator* by Roger M. Schwarz. In his book he indicates that

> group facilitation is a process in which a person who is acceptable to all members of the group, substantively neutral, and has no decision-making authority intervenes to help a group improve the way it identifies and solves problems and makes decisions, in order to increase the group's effectiveness.[3]

The basic job of the facilitator is to help the group improve its process and its overall effectiveness.

Schwarz makes a helpful distinction between *basic facilitation* and *developmental facilitation*. He indicates that in basic facilitation the group can influence the ongoing process at will, yet it depends on the facilitator to directly guide the group process. During developmental facilitation group members more actively observe and guide their own process while expecting the facilitator to be there to instruct them on how to become better facilitators themselves. In one sense it is simply "on-the-job training" for group members. The following Diagnosis-Intervention Cycle, which he presents in his book, is an excellent summary of where and when a group facilitator may want to intervene in the group process.[4]

Diagnosis-Intervention Cycle

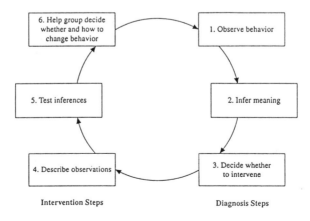

It will be helpful to keep the preceding chart in mind as you consider the many basic skills for effective group leadership that are described in the next section.

Basic Skills for Effective Group Leadership

Basic skills for effective leadership in groups include:

1. An ability to *listen* to others.

2. An ability to *summarize* where the group is.

3. An ability to *ask questions* in specific ways to guide the group in a needed direction.

4. An ability to *cope with conflict* when it arises and/or a willingness to elicit a hidden conflict when the group is avoiding it.

5. An ability to *be patient* when the group needs to struggle with an issue (without being rescued by a leader).

6. An ability to *distinguish* between our personal needs as leaders and the needs of the group.

7. An ability to *share leadership* functions within the group without being threatened that he or she will lose control of the group.

8. An ability to *facilitate* one member relating her or his contribution to another's idea in order to keep the discussion "building" in one direction.

9. An ability to *deal with* ideas, tasks, and feelings and develop a sense of timing as to when the *maintenance* of the group's life should be given priority over content or task.

10. An ability to be *comfortable* with group silence.

11. An ability to keep the group *focused on issues* rather than on personality.

12. An ability to help the group to do *problem solving and evaluation*.

13. An ability to *delegate responsibility*.

14. An ability to facilitate the group facing its own need to *terminate* when its task is finished.

15. An ability to enable the group to *set goals and revise* its goals when necessary.

16. An ability to enable the group to *understand* its own group processes and to learn from them.

Understanding Member Roles: Task and Maintenance

Above all, an effective group leader needs to facilitate the group members' understanding of the *task* and *maintenance roles* needed to help a group be effective. A group, like an individual, needs the knowledge, skills, and equipment its job calls for. It also needs to be in good working condition—willing to work, confident, and alert. If a group is to reach and maintain high productivity, its members have to provide for two kinds of needs—what it takes to do the job and what it takes to strengthen and maintain the group. These are functions that help to make the group cohesive.

Task Roles (functions required in selecting and carrying out a group task)

1. *Initiating Activity:* Proposing solutions; suggesting new ideas, new definitions of the problem, new attacks on the problem or new organization of material.

2. *Seeking Information:* Asking for clarification of suggestions, requesting additional information or facts.

3. *Seeking Opinion:* Looking for an expression of feeling about something from the members; seeking clarification of values, suggestions, or ideas.

4. *Giving Information:* Offering facts or generalizations, relating one's own experience to the group problem to illustrate a point.

5. *Giving Opinion:* Stating an opinion or belief concerning a suggestion or one of several suggestions, particularly concerning its value rather than its factual basis.

6. *Elaborating:* Clarifying, giving examples or developing meanings, trying to envision how a proposal might work out if adopted.

7. *Coordinating:* Showing relationships among various ideas or suggestions, trying to pull ideas and suggestions together, trying to draw together activities of various subgroups or members.

8. *Summarizing:* Pulling together related ideas or suggestions,

restating suggestions after the group has discussed them.

9. *Testing Feasibility:* Making application of suggestions to real situations, examining practicality and workability of ideas, pre-evaluating decisions.

Group Building or Group Maintenance Roles (functions required in strengthening and maintaining a group's life and helping it to stay together when the going is rough)

1. *Encouraging:* Being friendly, warm, responsive to others, praising others and their ideas, agreeing with and accepting contributions of others.

2. *Gate Keeping:* Trying to make it possible for another member to make a contribution to the group by saying, "We haven't heard anything from Jim yet," or suggesting a limited talking time for everyone so that all will have a chance to be heard.

3. *Standard Setting:* Expressing standards for the group to use in choosing its content or procedures or in evaluating its decisions, reminding the group to avoid decisions that conflict with group standards.

4. *Following:* Going along with decisions of the group, somewhat passively accepting ideas of others, serving as audience during group discussion and decision making.

5. *Expressing Group Feeling:* Summarizing what group feeling is sensed to be, describing reactions of the group to ideas or solutions.

Both Group Task and Group Maintenance Roles

1. *Evaluating:* Submitting group decisions or accomplishments for comparison with group norms, measuring accomplishments against goals.

2. *Diagnosing:* Determining sources of difficulties, appropriate steps to take next, the main blocks to progress.

3. *Testing for Consensus:* Tentatively asking for group opinions in order to find out if the group is nearing consensus on a decision, sending up trial balloons to test group opinions.

4. *Mediating:* Harmonizing, reconciling differences in points of

view, making compromise solutions.

5. *Relieving Tension:* Draining off negative feeling by joking or attempting to defuse a conflict, putting a tense situation in wider context.

6. *Understanding Acceptance of Expressed Feelings:* Freeing for further insight and participation.

The above list describes a range of behaviors that members of a group and the leader need to provide if the group is to be productive and satisfying. Any group is strengthened and enabled to work more effectively if the members:

1. Become conscious of the functional roles the group needs at any one time.

2. Find out the degree to which they are helping to meet these needs through what they do.

3. Undertake effective self-training to improve their member role behavior.

The "Task and Maintenance Functions" training workshop (Workshop 2) in chapter 7 can be useful in teaching a group these member roles. The accompanying chart in that section can help a group check on the way it is functioning.

Chapter 2

Stages of Group Development

The effective leader or facilitator of small groups needs to understand the context of the group, something about group norms, the task and maintenance functions that help a group do its work, and basic communication skills. A knowledge of the stages of group development and theoretical group models is basic for any leader.

Stages of Group Development

Groups go through predictable stages of development. A number of group theorists have developed organized steps outlining a group's development over a period of time. Although small-group leaders or facilitators are sometimes confused when certain things occur in a group, these are usually normal aspects of that group's growth. If one can understand some of the normal developmental steps through which a group struggles, then what often seems unusual or confusing behavior can be viewed as a routine step.

For example, most groups experience some degree of struggle over who will be the leader and who will influence the group significantly. Even if the group has an official leader or chairperson, it is quite possible for others in the group to lead the group via informal means of influence. One form of informal influence is to create doubt through the use of questions or silence. Such informal influence may or may not serve to undermine the leadership role of the designated leader or facilitator. Of course, direct, open influence on a group is ideal and to be encouraged by all group members. It is helpful to a group for persons to indicate an open desire to influence the group discussion or decision-making process.

Group Process: A Developmental Perspective

A recent model that is helpful in showing a more integrative model of group development has been published by Susan A. Wheelan in a book entitled *Group Processes: A Developmental Perspective.*[1] Her five-stage model encompasses the following stages:

Stage One: Dependency and Inclusion

Stage Two: Counterdependency and Fight

Stage Three: Trust and Structure

Stage Four: Work

Stage Five: Termination

Stage One is the first stage of group development, in which members rely greatly on the *group's leader.* The group depends on the leader for direction, safety, acceptance, and structure. Members tend to respect the leader's authority and rarely challenge the designated leader. People have an initial need to be included in the group and will not risk rejection and alienation.

Stage Two is the stage wherein the group dynamic is characterized by *counterdependence and fights.* Conflict among members or between leader and member(s) is typical and to be expected. Experts indicate that a stage of conflict is necessary for a group to develop cohesion. If conflict is avoided or denied, the group may never develop any cohesion or ability to work together. In this instance, the group never fully develops and thus remains stuck in stage two. The basic task in this stage is to clarify how the group will operate, what roles each one will take, what responsibility and/or authority each will take, how decisions are to be made, and when and how assignments will be implemented.

Given the complexity of all this role clarification, the possibility for misunderstandings, power struggles, and conflict is great. The energy in conflict may be used to allow the group to clarify and settle real differences, or it may block the group from further development.

Conflict Defined

Conflict is defined as *dealing with differences.* It does not have to be an emotional shouting match, only an honest facing of differences. Yes, it is something to worry about if your group never experiences any differences or tensions and people seem to always get along and agree on everything. That is too perfect for reality. Without conflict, it is difficult to develop trust in others. If we feel we can get along only by agreeing all the time and never sharing any deeper or different feelings, values, or beliefs, we are deceiving ourselves. What kind of relationship or group do we have if only positive things can be shared? If we can't trust a range of human feelings and experiences with one another, then on what level do we develop trust?

Conflict Utilization

Previously, I wrote that

interpersonal conflict . . . has tended to be valued as negative . . . It is consistent, then, to place the emphasis on conflict resolution rather than on conflict utilization. *Utilization* suggests that productive conflict . . . will energize . . . interactions and contribute to problem solving and problem resolution rather than repression of needful conflict. Certainly, destructive conflicts are needless and to be avoided if at all possible.[2]

Conflict can be productive and even positive when dealt with properly.

Verbal Confrontation

It is common for the group to confront or challenge the leader during this stage as well as one another. Please note: such verbal assertions are normative in this stage and should not be personalized by either leader or members! If you feel angry or defensive over such attacks, be aware that you may be angry over being treated on an *impersonal* rather than a personal basis.

Simply put, conflict, verbal attacks, confrontation, and emotionality are all normative and a necessary part of all small-group development. Without it, groups never fully develop. Is it any surprise that some groups seem boring, flat, lacking direction, or overly intellectual and impersonal? No wonder! They have undoubtedly avoided any stage-two conflict or differences. If one desires to lead a small group, learn about stage-two dynamics; then expect or even encourage some conflict or dealing with differences.

Stage Three deals with *trust and structure*. With a conflictual stage two behind them, group members can begin to feel more trusting of one another. The atmosphere becomes more relaxed; communication is more open and spontaneous. Group norms and standards are more readily clarified, and feedback begins to be a regular part of the process of interacting with others.

At this stage, it begins to be clear that all group members represent resources of experience, knowledge, expertise, and ability to assume various assignments or work roles. Clearly the group is preparing for work as it plans and prepares for stage four.

Stage Four is the time when *work* occurs. Effective groups and leaders share ideas and information, exchange feedback with one another, complete their jobs if there is a job to perform within a given time line.

It has been estimated that functional groups spend approximately 60 percent of their time on work (task) and about 40 percent of their time on relational and interpersonal issues (maintenance).

A key to an effective group is the utilization of its resources. If some members are devalued or rejected by the group, no matter how important their contribution may be, the group deprives itself of some of its human resources and robs itself of potentially enriching contributions from the devalued members.

Stage Five is the *termination* phase. During the termination phase, group members need to begin to debrief all that they have experienced. They need encouragement to discuss the anticipated ending. A group leader can facilitate their discussion of individual future plans. Feelings about separation, ending, or unfinished business need to be dealt with at this time. An overview of the group's total life together, complete with its successes and achievements, is important to verbalize.

In religious and voluntary organizations, most groups have a time line by which they need to terminate. Membership on a board or committee usually carries a clear tenure of one to three years. Classes often meet for no more than nine months to a year. Other groups are more temporary yet need clear guidelines at the beginning regarding how long they will function, to whom they are accountable, who is the leader, and when and how they will terminate.

Whenever groups near termination, they tend to regress to an earlier stage of group development as they anticipate ending and separating. There can be a *cycle of small regressions* along with a *small series of advances* all mixed together during the latter part of the termination stage. Such a cycle of seeming contradictions is normative for most small groups approaching their final time together.

A feeling of some distance from others in the group with whom one has felt close is typical of the pattern of termination. All feelings of distance are typical of this final stage and are not to be seen as unusual or to be taken personally. A distant feeling at this stage is not the same as concluding that the other person no longer likes me. Distance is simply a necessary "spacer" for the time to come when we will not be seeing one another again on a regular basis. It is easy to misinterpret or misunderstand the need for distance at this stage.

Stage Five Termination Characteristics

Dr. Wheelan reports the following list of characteristics for a Stage Five group nearing termination:[3]

1. Group members know that the group will be ending soon.

2. The group's ability to manage conflict may begin to degenerate.

3. Members may discuss ways to continue the group beyond its designated ending point.

4. Work activity may increase or decrease abruptly.

5. Feelings of solidarity among members may increase.

6. Increased expressions of positive feelings among members may occur.

7. Problematic issues may be avoided.

8. Stress and anxiety among members are evident.

9. Some members may become apathetic with regard to the group.

10. Members discuss group achievements.

One Way to View a Group: The I.C.A. Theory

One of the best-known theories about how groups develop is called the I.C.A. theory. The letters represent *inclusion, control,* and *affection*, and the theory was developed by William C. Schutz. Let us now consider this theory as one way to view a group as it develops.

Schutz stated in his I.C.A. theory that all persons have three interpersonal needs when functioning within a small group. The three interpersonal needs are *inclusion, control, and affection.*[4]

Because these three needs operate within persons, Schutz felt that small groups must have the same three needs of inclusion, control, and affection functioning within the group. An alternate set of descriptive words might be acceptance, influence, and expression of strong feelings. Over the years he discovered through his research that groups actually do move through these three stages of development. Schutz also discovered that as a group begins to wind down and conclude its work, *the stages reverse themselves:* affection, control, and inclusion. So the overview of the stages a group moves through may now be viewed as the following steps: inclusion (I), control (C), and affection (A) followed by the reverse cycle of affection (A), control (C), and inclusion (I).

By knowing this sequence of developmental steps, a group leader or facilitator may anticipate certain dynamics and group problems. Certainly the group leader will understand that a group must go through the various steps of growth if it is to develop fully as a group. It is possible, however, for a group never to develop beyond the first step of inclusion (I). Such groups are often described as "failures" or "disappointing" experiences by both members and leaders. The following diagram portrays the various steps in the I.C.A. theory in graphic fashion.

The Inclusion-Control-Affection Theory

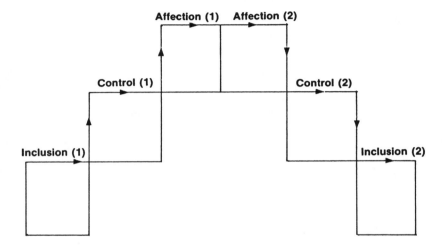

by William Schutz
(Diagram by N. W. Turner)

According to Schutz, the basic concerns of a group will focus on inclusion, control, and affection. When people in a group begin to focus on any one of these three concerns, the following questions illustrate the concerns shared in a typical group:[5]

Inclusion:
Who else is here?
How can I be in relationship to them?
What will it cost to join this group?
How much am I willing to pay to become a member?
Can I trust my real self to them?
Will they support me if the going gets rough?
How can I get acquainted with them?

Control:

Who is calling the shots here?

How much can I push for what I want?

Will I have to be direct or indirect to influence others?

What do others require of me?

Can I say what I really think and feel?

Can I take it if they say what they really think?

Affection:

Am I willing to care?

Can I show my caring?

What will happen if I show I care for one person before I show caring for others?

What if no one cares for me?

What if they do show caring for me?

What if I don't really ever care for someone in the group?

Will the group be able to bear it?

Is showing affection acceptable in this group? How do I know?

The I.C.A. way of viewing a group is a practical way to examine a church or voluntary board, committee, or small group. Voluntary organizations and church groups are similar; meetings begin with members having the concerns listed under the inclusion section above. Certainly questions like "Who is here," "What is your name," and "Can I trust myself with this group" are typical concerns in any church organization. Control concerns usually arise with questions like "Who is leading the meeting today?" and "How much will this group require of me?" Affectional concerns normally surface with questions like "Will the others in this group like me?" and "Can I dare show caring for another member when we are to be focused only on the task before us?"

When a group knows that its life must terminate, for instance, in a board or committee at the end of the program year when some members' terms of office will be up, the I.C.A. process tends to reverse itself as A.C.I. During this closing-out process, we usually see persons beginning to pull back from affectional ties that will have no future beyond the group, and we see control concerns arise again, expressed by "Who's boss here?" or "You don't have the right to make that decision now!" Finally, the inclusion concern arises again around questions of whether we want to put time into the future efforts of this class, group, board, or committee.

In viewing a group from the I.C.A. framework, it is important to realize that all these concerns overlap during the life of a group. This is especially so if a new member enters the group, a member leaves, or the group experiences a trauma. Certainly one of the three concerns may predominate, yet the other two concerns may be in evidence in minor or subtle ways.

Chapter 3

Leadership in Groups

Leadership can occasionally be a confusing term. What does it really mean? What are its implications in small groups? Is leadership always carried out by a certain kind of person?

Leadership is traditionally considered to be exercised by a certain type of person leading a group in a particular manner. The usual types of leadership roles within groups or organizations include president, vice-president, secretary, and treasurer. Clearly, authority is traditionally vested in the specific leader role or position. Additional leadership roles include those of facilitator, teacher, convener, or chairperson.

Leadership is a *function* of specific influence occurring within a group. Leadership is a particular *role* assigned, delegated, or given by others in the group to a person or persons within a group or organization. Leadership is a *process* involving two or more persons in a group for the purpose of attaining common goals. Leadership is a set of *interpersonal skills* learned or acquired by a person who is interested in developing his or her ability to influence others. Finally, leadership assumes an ability to *communicate clearly* with others and to be able to cope with the mutual dependency engendered between leader and followers.

In order to be clear on what this chapter is about, let us clarify that leadership is primarily a function and responsibility of the *total group*. Consequently, a group may function without an official leader (often called a "leaderless" group) and perform very well indeed. Chapter 1 details many of the basic leadership functions provided by members in a group if effective work is to be done. A major shift in the field of social psychology in recent years affirms the view that leadership is a set of learned skills rather than a set of characteristics bestowed on one person alone. For years churches and religious institutions have been oriented toward dramatic types of leaders who can preach, teach, lead, and/or entertain persons with their "charisma." The dependence of religious groups and organizations on such personality types fostered an era of feeling that "our group cannot meet or decide anything until our leader arrives." A new era began some years ago with the use of leaderless groups, the employment of varied small-group methods (like meeting in twos, threes, or fours), and the acceptance of the idea that leadership is a group responsibility.

The theory of *functional leadership* contains two basic ideas: (1) any member of the group may assume the leadership of the group by performing actions that fulfill group functional needs, and (2) every leadership function may be fulfilled by a variety of group members serving various group needs with their specific behaviors (like asking questions or making supportive statements).

Lewin, Lippitt, and White are known for their research on three leadership styles, which they named *autocratic, democratic,* and *laissez-faire.* The *autocratic* leader decided all policy and gave all orders to group members. The *democratic* leader encouraged group determination of policy and enabled the group to interact within itself. The *laissez-faire* leader provided very minimal leadership for the group and interacted with group members in only a marginal or average manner. Most of the research upheld the democratic leadership style as the most effective. Yet different leadership styles seem to be effective under different conditions.

There is a relationship between the above research and other leadership studies performed by Fred Fiedler, a social psychologist. He discovered that task-oriented and maintenance-oriented leaders performed better according to the needs in a specific situation. He did not find that one type of leadership orientation was effective in all situations. In other words, leadership style and orientation are most effective when performed in direct response to a specific situation and group need. For example, a task-oriented leader, one who has a concern that the agenda be completed or the lesson for the day taught, functions best when on good terms with the group, when the task to be done is clearly structured, and when the leader commands significant power and authority in the group. The task-oriented leader is also effective when the leader directs the group and/or assumes responsibility for making decisions. In contrast, a maintenance-oriented leader is most effective when encouraging decision making by broad involvement of the group members. Clearly, situational and contextual differences in groups need to be allowed for in determining what kind of leadership orientation and style would be most helpful. An effective leader will be flexible enough to adjust herself or himself to the group and will seek a balance between task completion and maintenance needs, such as how people are feeling about doing the task. Group dynamics are far too complex for any one theory or style of group leadership to be effective under all conditions.

Identifying One's Leadership Style

In order to be an effective group leader, it is important to assess one's own leadership style. It is appropriate to ask: Am I more task oriented or maintenance oriented? Do I have a reasonable balance in my own leadership style between the need to get the task done and the need to maintain the life of the group? Do I feel more comfortable with one orientation than the other? If so, what influence does my orientation have on the group(s) I lead?

Additional questions that need to be asked are: Am I predominantly a democratic, autocratic, or laissez-faire type of leader? What does this type of leadership style do to the group(s) I lead? Am I comfortable with my style, or do I want to make some changes in my style? What type of feedback and/or evaluation do I request about my style from groups I lead? How do I feel about being evaluated as a leader? Do I practice what I ask of others? Does a group's reluctance to evaluate itself or me suggest anything special to me about its dynamics?

A person who has developed a democratic style of leadership is most likely one who usually maintains an adequate balance between task and maintenance orientation. If there is an imbalance toward too much maintenance, the designated leader may be leaning toward a laissez-faire style. An imbalance toward too much task orientation may mean the leader is risking autocratic tendencies.

In approaching how to conduct and lead a small-group discussion, the following list of ten items with a graphic illustration may be a helpful resource to the reader:

Conducting the Discussion[1]

1. Help the group to make adequate preparation for the discussion by reading resource material. Establish connections between background materials, and the experience of group members.

2. Aim at the outset to get a sharply defined question before the group. Have three or four alternatives.

3. In general, don't put questions to particular group members, unless you see that an idea is trying to find expression: "Mrs. Brown, you were about to say something."

4. Interrupt the "speech maker" as tactfully as possible: "I think you've made your point, John. Now let's hear from some of the others."

5. Keep the discussion meaningful. Avoid unproductive sidetracks.

Goes this way:

Not this way:

6. The leader should avoid dominating the discussion and should encourage others to voice their ideas.

7. If some important angle is being neglected, point it out.

8. Encourage ease, informality, good humor. Foster friendly disagreement.

9. Take time occasionally to draw loose ends together. "Let's see where we're going." Close a discussion with a summary.

10. Help the group to discover unanswered questions for future study and action.

Twenty-Verbs Exercise

In a recent book, *Joining Together: Group Theory and Group Skills*, the following exercise was included to enable persons to evaluate their degree of sociability and dominance in interacting with other group members. The instructions are as follows:[2]

There are twenty verbs listed below that describe some of the ways in which people feel and act from time to time. Think of your behavior in groups. How do you feel and act? Check five verbs below that best describe your behavior in groups as you see it.

In a group, I:

_____ Acquiesce	_____ Concur	_____ Lead
_____ Advise	_____ Criticize	_____ Oblige
_____ Agree	_____ Direct	_____ Relinquish
_____ Analyze	_____ Disapprove	_____ Resist
_____ Assist	_____ Evade	_____ Retreat
_____ Concede	_____ Initiate	_____ Withdraw
_____ Coordinate	_____ Judge	

Two underlying factors or traits are involved in the list of verbs: *dominance* (authority or control) and *sociability* (intimacy or friendliness). Most people tend to like to control things (high dominance) or to let others control things (low dominance). Similarly, most people tend to be warm and personal (high sociability) or to be somewhat cold and impersonal (low sociability). In the following chart, circle the five verbs you used to describe yourself in group activity. The box in which three or more verbs are circled out of the five represents your interpersonal pattern tendency in groups.

	HIGH DOMINANCE	LOW DOMINANCE
HIGH SOCIABILITY	advise coordinate direct initiate lead	acquiesce agree assist oblige concur
LOW SOCIABILITY	analyze criticize disapprove judge resist	concede evade relinquish retreat withdraw

After determining your dominance-sociability pattern in groups, ask yourself if it is the kind of pattern you want. If not, why not? Are you willing to risk changing?

Analyzing Interpersonal Interactions

One skill a leader needs is an awareness of how persons are interacting within the group process. Robert Bales of Harvard University developed a verbal observation system for persons to observe the extent to which task and maintenance functions actually occur within the group's process. He named it the "Interaction Process Analysis System." Readers will note a similarity to Bales's list and the group member task/maintenance functions in chapter 1. The emphasis here, however, is on the role of the designated leader, teacher, facilitator, chairperson, and so forth.[3]

As you can see in Figure 1, the first three categories are positive emotions, while the final three categories represent negative feelings. Categories 4, 5, and 6 stand for task functions that are given

Figure 1

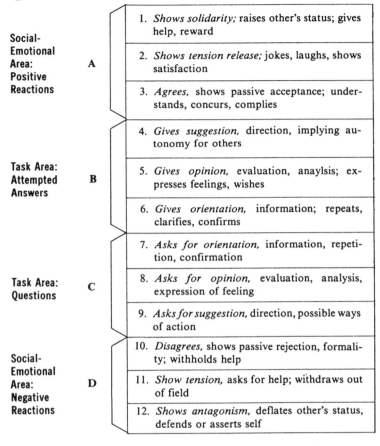

Social-Emotional Area: Positive Reactions	A	1. *Shows solidarity;* raises other's status; gives help, reward
		2. *Shows tension release;* jokes, laughs, shows satisfaction
		3. *Agrees,* shows passive acceptance; understands, concurs, complies
Task Area: Attempted Answers	B	4. *Gives suggestion,* direction, implying autonomy for others
		5. *Gives opinion,* evaluation, anaylsis; expresses feelings, wishes
		6. *Gives orientation,* information; repeats, clarifies, confirms
Task Area: Questions	C	7. *Asks for orientation,* information, repetition, confirmation
		8. *Asks for opinion,* evaluation, analysis, expression of feeling
		9. *Asks for suggestion,* direction, possible ways of action
Social-Emotional Area: Negative Reactions	D	10. *Disagrees,* shows passive rejection, formality; withholds help
		11. *Show tension,* asks for help; withdraws out of field
		12. *Shows antagonism,* deflates other's status, defends or asserts self

to a group, while categories 7, 8, and 9 represent task functions that ask for assistance from others. This blend of task and social-emotional verbal behaviors is very close to the task and maintenance behaviors mentioned in the previous chapter. One interesting feature of Bales's system is that the categories are polar opposites; namely, categories 1 and 12 are opposites, categories 2 and 11 are opposites, and so forth.

A leader or a group interested in objectively analyzing how well it meets its goals or does its work will find it helpful to identify the task and maintenance verbal behaviors within its process. The Bales Interaction Process Analysis can be utilized either by observers of the process or by the group itself using a tape recorder to review its behavior. By tallying the number of different types of comments (see tally form in Figure 2 below) made within a thirty-minute period, a group can begin an objective analysis of its task and maintenance (social/emotional) patterns. Another approach is to observe a leader or a group in order to identify specific patterns of task/maintenance verbal behaviors.[3]

Figure 2[4]

	0%	10%	20%	30%	40%	50%
1. *Shows solidarity,* raises other's status, gives help, reward.						
2. *Shows tension release,* jokes, laughs, shows satisfaction.						
3. *Agrees,* shows passive acceptance, understands, concurs, complies.						
4. *Gives suggestion,* direction, implying autonomy for others.						
5. *Gives opinion,* evaluation, analysis; expresses feeling, wish.						
6. *Gives orientation,* information, repeats, clarifies, confirms.						
7. *Asks for orientation,* information, repetition, confirmation.						
8. *Asks for opinion,* evaluation, analysis, expression of feeling.						
9. *Asks for suggestion,* direction, possible ways of action.						
10. *Disagrees,* shows passive rejection, formality, withholds help.						
11. *Shows tension,* asks for help, withdraws out of field.						
12. *Shows antagonism,* deflates other's status, defends or asserts self.						

Persons doing even a brief analysis of their group's verbal behaviors will learn whether there is a balance between task and social-emotional comments occurring in the group. A lack of balance may serve to explain why the group is not doing its job well.

Leadership in Organizations

Leadership within organizations may call for a variety of leadership styles. Leadership may be formal or informal, authoritative or democratic, supervisory or supportive. It may be rewarding or punishing by either direct or indirect means. Religious organizations tend to specialize in indirect methods of leadership in order to avoid direct confrontation and/or open conflict in interpersonal relationships.

A facilitator's style directly influences group functioning. It is crucial that a leader assess her or his impact on group functioning rather than blame the group for being ineffective.

The following chart is a graphic way of showing that when a leader shares decision-making responsibility with the group, the group increases its participation in making decisions and taking responsibility for them. To use the chart, begin reading with item 1 on the left and move toward item 7 on the right. You will see that as the role of the leader becomes one of sharing (and changing leadership style), the role of the group increases in responsibility and in participation. The diagonal line also graphically portrays this shift in responsibility.

Leadership Behavior in Making Decisions[5]

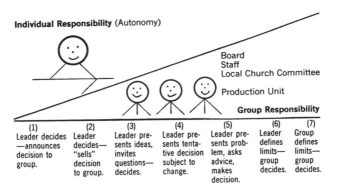

(1)	(2)	(3)	(4)	(5)	(6)	(7)
Leader decides —announces decision to group.	Leader decides— "sells" decision to group.	Leader presents ideas, invites questions— decides.	Leader presents tentative decision subject to change.	Leader presents problem, asks advice, makes decision.	Leader defines limits— group decides.	Group defines limits— group decides.

Leadership Training for Small Groups

Religious organizations and other voluntary organizations need to train their small-group leaders and facilitators in a range of skills. I offer the following suggestions for what should be included in leadership training as some that I have discovered from personal experience and professional training:

1. Understand the nature of small-group dynamics.

2. Obtain a general knowledge of the stages of small-group development.

3. Learn about the life cycle of groups and organizations and the necessity of planned termination for most groups.

4. Develop a broad vision for the variety and scope of small groups a church or voluntary organization needs to consider offering.

5. Learn how to contract for the group purpose, time line, leadership, resources, membership criteria, and termination process for each small group.

6. Develop skills and knowledge in group problem-solving and decision-making processes.

7. Study and practice conflict utilization skills as a small-group facilitator.

8. Develop and practice small-group facilitator skills until you are comfortable with them.

9. Understand and practice task and maintenance roles as a small-group leader.

Part of the training of small-group leaders may include an awareness of some group procedures used with larger audiences as well as smaller "buzz groups." The following charts graphically portray the functioning of (1) buzz groups, (2) group discussion, (3) panel discussion, and (4) a symposium.[6]

1. Description	2. Advantages	3. Limitations

Buzz Groups

1. Encouraging large groups to participate in discussion by dividing the group into smaller groups to discuss a particular topic and then report back to the larger group.

2. Promotes enthusiasm and involvement as it provides opportunity for maximum discussion in limited time.

3. Discussion tends to be shallow, disorganized, and easily dominated by one or two in the group; needs skillful leader to handle the process.

Group
Discussion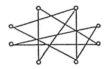

1. Two or more persons sharing knowledge, experiences, and opinions, building on ideas, clarifying, evaluating, and coordinating to reach an agreement or gain better understanding.

2. Meets the needs of group members by providing high degree of interaction, interest, and involvement.

3. Does not provide authoritative information nor is it helpful for large groups; requires time, patience, and capable leadership.

Panel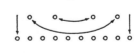

X

1. Discussing an issue among three or more persons before a group under the direction of a moderator, followed by group discussion.

2. Presents different viewpoints to stimulate thinking.

3. Needs skillful moderator to keep panel on subject and limited number of questioners from monopolizing the discussion; needs a balanced panel to keep personalities from influencing opinions.

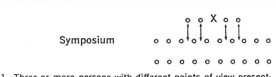

Symposium

1. Three or more persons with different points of view present-
   ing short speeches followed by questions and answers
   under the direction of a moderator.

2. Presents several viewpoints and, through questions, clari-
   fies information to meet specific needs.

3. Requires speakers with equal ability, a skillful chairman,
   and freedom of participation.

Charismatic Leaders

Webster's New Collegiate Dictionary defines charisma as "an extraordinary power (as of healing) given a Christian by the Holy Spirit for the good of the church; a personal magic of leadership arousing special popular loyalty or enthusiasm for a public figure; a special magnetic charm or appeal." Research tends to show that leaders with charisma have a vision others find compelling and that they are able to recruit others who share the vision. Their relationship with members enables them to persuade people to work for and with the vision. Charisma is a gift, and it can be positive and does make some real contributions. Yet charisma can turn negative and even destructive in human relationships. Specifically, when charisma is combined with narcissism, it becomes negative and eventually abusive or destructive for group members or followers. (In discussing charisma, we are not referring to the so-called charismatic movement within church and religious circles.) The field of religion has always had its share of leaders with charisma. Religion has also had its share of narcissistic leaders who had some form of charisma and abused their power over their adherents.

Following the Leader

The following list from a recent journal article lists the steps from the followers' perspective with narcissistic charismatic leaders:[7]

Step One: We idolize our leader.

Step Two: We are asked to support our leader's vision, direction, interpretation.

Step Three: We continue to idolize our leader.

Step Four: We comply with conviction.

Step Five: We bolster our leader's strength.

Step Six: We do not fully succeed and thus let him/her down.

Step Seven: We are blamed.

Step Eight: We internalize the blame.

Step Nine: We listen only to the leader.

Not all group or organizational leaders are even consciously aware of their abuse of their followers. Their lack of awareness is in fact one of their major problems. Followers tend to collude with the leaders and accept blame for failures even when they are not responsible. Their need is to continue to perpetuate the myth of a perfect, wonderful, and charming leader to whom they feel an often blind loyalty.

In the field of religion, churches, and other voluntary organizations, small groups are often a major means of inducing more and more members to adore a leader who is charming, entertaining, visionary, exciting, and loaded with charisma.

Leader Failings

Leaders seem to fail most often in their ability to work with and through others to build a team and accomplish goals in a collaborative manner. Many failures come from a character weakness that alienates others and prevents them from working cooperatively and easily with others.

So-called dark-side characteristics—that is, irritating tendencies that alienate others—are often disguised and hidden and difficult to detect. Some people, including people with charisma and charm, interview well and cover over any dark-side characteristics. It is easy, then, for organizations to secure a leader who will fail over time when the dark-side characteristics emerge. The famous psychiatrist Carl Jung called this our "shadow side."

Small-Group Dangers

If your organization is thinking of forming small groups, is perfect attendance required? Why or why not? Is confidentiality required? Why or why not? Are your questions regarded as an act of disloyalty to the group? Why or why not? Is group membership closed to outsiders once the group is formed? Is there a time limit for the group after which it disbands, or is it an open-ended group? How will it be decided to add or subtract members? Who makes that decision? Is the purpose of the small group and its membership open knowledge to the total organization? Is the group purpose consistent with the overall mission of the church, voluntary, or larger organization?

If you have difficulty answering these questions or the nine steps of narcissistic leaders cited earlier felt familiar, be aware that you may be falling under your leader's charm and charisma. Be aware that no one can change such a leader—and it is better to find another leader or disband the group.

Chapter 4

Creative Use of Conflict

Most of us usually regard conflict as a negative thing. Within the Christian church we are taught to value peace very highly. Biblically, we are enjoined to forgive others. Repentance, reconciliation, and atonement are familiar terms to church members. Preachers admonish persons for hating, while affirming those who love. Anger is regarded as a "no-no." Hostility between persons is regarded negatively. Conflict in marriage and the family is bad because we are supposed to love and support one another. Conflict within the church is unthinkable, since it appears to contradict our loving heritage. Even more revealing of our values is the minimal amount of material written about conflict by religious institutions and leadership.

The church is not alone in this. Most voluntary organizations usually thrive on goodwill and positive images of the people they serve. Conflict, therefore, is viewed as negative by most organizations that want to grow and thrive in our culture!

Nevertheless, conflict has been occurring within Christendom and the rest of the world for centuries in both direct and indirect forms. It is time for church groups and voluntary organizations to acknowledge what has been, is, and will be happening regarding conflict within their ranks. Indeed, it is dehumanizing to deny that a church has conflict and to see the same church split or die years later. The very existence of the biblical themes of forgiveness, reconciliation, repentance, and atonement reveal that human beings experience conflict. Perhaps our greatest sins are denial and rationalization.

Conflict occurs whenever people fail to agree on anything. Dealing with conflict begins by recognizing that we have differences. And how we handle our differences says a lot about how we will cope with conflict. Church groups tend to cope poorly and uncreatively with conflict. The purpose of this chapter is to share a few ideas on how conflict may be used in a creative way.

Leaders in religious and other voluntary organizations are usually persons who give their time and energy freely to the organization. Since volunteers donate their time, it is difficult to make demands on them and enforce the normative organizational authority that one usually has in a business organization with paid employees who can be hired and fired. The mixture of paid professional staff directing the efforts of unpaid volunteer staff does not make for the easiest or clearest of working relationships. Add in assumptions regarding often unarticulated and unclear expectations, fuzzy job descriptions for paid staff, and demands placed on volunteer members of boards and committees, and we have the beginnings of potential conflict. Factor in the attrition and turnover rate of volunteer leaders in an organization, and we have an even greater potential for conflict. And, with the recent trend in corporate America to downsize and lay off thousands of people simultaneously, the sense of job security is disappearing in the nation. With such a loss of control over one's career and future employability, it is not surprising that some members of religious groups and other voluntary organizations experience a need to feel in control of something somewhere. It will not be unusual to see religious and voluntary organizations beginning to encounter an increase in leadership struggles for power and control positions within their organizational life.

Churches and voluntary organizations need to prepare for increased conflicts arising from understandable power and control needs that are no longer satisfied in the working world during the week. These conflicts need to be dealt with early on! Delay and denial serve only to increase the seriousness of conflict later on. Conflict can be costly. And the longer it is avoided, the more it usually costs us. Waiting does not make it go away. Waiting only drives it deeper down, and when it does surface, it usually is bigger and more frightening than before.

Clergy and other professional staff are well-meaning persons who usually seek "peace at any price." The trend these days is that the "price of peace has increased with inflation." Premature conflict resolution that fails to resolve all underlying issues is no bargain. In fact, it serves only to put things off for a larger, more destructive and costly scenario later. When will we learn that by delaying our dealing with a conflict, we contribute to a self-fulfilling prophecy that helps make real our worst fears—that conflict is terrible and should be avoided at all costs!

Culture and Value Changes

Changes in the nation's culture will continue to contribute to diversity and differences evidenced in most churches, religious institutions, and voluntary organizations. As diversity increases, so will the different needs of diverse peoples increase.

Traditional values that deny or avoid conflict are now on a collision course with newer values advocating strong stands on social issues, including racial and ethnic discrimination, gender equality, and a renewed emphasis on the rights of children and the aging, who are often subtly discriminated against. Potential conflict is always around the corner these days—or so it seems.

Leader Roles and System Dynamics

The role of clergy and leaders in voluntary and nonprofit organizations places them in an inevitable position to be either the object of criticism and conflict or the advocate of a social issue or cause that will eventually lead to some form of conflict. Expectations placed on leaders are increasing. Few leaders in such organizations can ever begin to meet all the various expectations of them. Failed expectations, even silent ones never articulated to leaders, lead to disappointment, criticism, and eventually conflict within the organization. It is imperative that a voluntary organization or local church, therefore, have a board or committee whose primary job is to be a neutral sounding board for all sides and a place to mediate feedback and open two-way communication between leaders and the rest of the people. The local church or volunteer organization needs to be viewed as an organizational system. Organizational systems generate their own system dynamics, which are largely impersonal and include some system conflicts. If leaders or staff personalize an impersonal *system dynamic* and conflict, they fail to understand the system dynamics and allow themselves to be enmeshed in a largely impersonal process. That is a mistake!

Just because a leader is accused of something *by name* does not make it personal—though it feels personal. Most members of organizations and businesses tend to blame the top executive for any or all problems, whether that CEO (chief executive officer) did anything wrong or not. Witness the increasing shorter job tenure for our nation's college presidents and corporate CEOs. The pastor is the equivalent of the CEO in a church. The pastor is usually the day-to-day manager of the church's business details and coordinator of church programs as well as many other arrangements such as staff meetings. Potential blame "comes with the territory," whether we like it or not.

Ten Ways for Leaders to Avoid Conflict

Let us consider some things for clergy and leaders of voluntary organizations to avoid in conflict situations:

1. Avoid personalizing everything said against you as the leader.

2. Avoid assuming that people have all the facts of the situation correct; in most cases people know only some of the facts of the total situation.

3. Avoid paranoia. Not everyone is against you.

4. Avoid the tendency to oversimplify and reduce things down to one or two variables when it is usually more complex.

5. Avoid polarization of the situation—we/they, I/you, win/lose.

6. Avoid becoming involved in secrets, secret meetings, agreeing to keep things confidential or anonymous, and so on in conflictive situations. Conflict thrives on secrecy and fades with openness and truth. Conflict flourishes when a complex situation is reduced to

one or two variables. Most situations are very complex, with more than just one or two variables occurring simultaneously.

7. Avoid assuming that all parties see the same thing the same way! Conflict often arises out of different perceptions of the same alleged scenario. How common it is to assume we know all when we only perceive one part!

8. Avoid becoming overly fearful, which causes us to lose hope.

9. Avoid assuming members come from the same culture, history, or background; churches and voluntary organizations have more diversity in membership than ever before.

10. Avoid getting trapped in triangles where you as a leader are the main conduit of communication between two other persons or focal points.

Conflict: Its Values and Varied Dimensions

Basic to our whole discussion is a need to examine our values. Unless we can value the creative use of conflict, we cannot creatively use its energy and cope with it. Fear will inhibit a group and reduce its problem-solving potential and its progress toward a goal.

> Verbal conflict is a process characterized by a state of group tension manifested by (1) verbal disagreements (over beliefs, attitudes, values, interests, and information); (2) competition; (3) personal attacks that injure self-esteem; (4) mutually exclusive goals; or (5) a refusal to cope with the preceding verbal conflict.[1]

Interpersonal conflict has *many dimensions and modes*. For example, a conflict may be triggered by an old "hidden agenda" (that is, old feelings held over from a prior meeting) that occurs within the present and carries implications for the future. Consequently, the conflict occurs in several time dimensions. The same conflict may also be expressed directly ("I am upset with you!") while the tone of voice communicates an indirect message ("I need you as a friend despite the momentary burst of anger."). With conflict's many dimensions, it is logical that we might experience varied types of conflict.

Types of Conflict

The following are the four most familiar types of conflict:

1. *Intrapersonal conflict.* This type of conflict occurs only within the individual. For example, if I have a conflict between two or more of my values, I have an intrapersonal conflict—it is within myself. One problem is that some persons occasionally allow (consciously or unconsciously) an intrapersonal conflict to trigger an interpersonal conflict (with another person) as a way to try to reduce his or her own internal pressures or unhappiness.

2. *Interpersonal conflict.* This type of conflict occurs between two or more persons. Typical examples would be a marital or family conflict. Or it might be a difference between two or more board, committee, or staff members.

3. *Intragroup conflict.* This type of conflict occurs within one group. For example, if a local church or voluntary organization's board or committee becomes involved in conflict over its own agenda items, it is experiencing intragroup conflict.

4. *Intergroup conflict.* This type of conflict occurs between two or more groups from the same voluntary organization or church. An example would be two committees disagreeing over who should receive a cut in the annual budget or which committee had the right to decide a specific policy for the organization, since both committees had partial responsibility for the same policy.

Positive and Negative Uses of Conflict

One researcher has noted that most problem-solving groups move through three stages of growth: (1) *orientation* (what is the problem?); (2) *evaluation* (how do we feel about it?); and (3) *control* (what can we do about it?). Conflict may occur at any stage of development, yet the control stage most often serves to trigger interpersonal conflict within a group.

Another researcher identifies the initial stage of development as a time of orientation and testing. The second stage, intergroup conflict, is characterized by hostility, defensiveness, tension, competition, and collapse of group structure. (See chapter 2 for further information.)

This background information is included to emphasize that most groups will (or may) go through a stage of conflict on their way to developing fully into a mature and effective group. Any attempt by the leadership to suppress, deny, avoid, or put down a stage of conflict may be a decision to stop the group from fully developing its potential. To deny or avoid potentially positive uses of conflict is a negative use of the group's power and potential.

Negative uses of conflict occur when persons are attacked, motives impugned, and emotionality used to cloud real issues.

Positive use of conflict within the group serves to clarify goals and boundaries for the group. A leadership struggle can have positive results when a group tests out what kind of authority it desires and with which type it best functions. Positive uses of conflict include focusing on issues, accepting without prejudging another's motives, and determining to work on one issue at a time without escalating issues together. Positive disagreements serve to clarify the parameters and dimensions of a problem that might be otherwise missed, overlooked, or avoided by rushing too fast!

Fourteen Options
for Leaders in Utilizing Conflict

Dealing with conflict can be a scary thing for anyone not trained or experienced in doing so. Since few of us ever have reason to receive formal training in dealing with conflict, what options are available to us when a conflict does arise?

A number of resource books in print offer practical help. Books such as *Moving Your Church Through Conflict* and others found in the bibliography of this book are good resources to consult.

It is important to decide whether one is going to cope with the conflict directly, avoid the conflict if possible, or act ambivalently about it. If one decides to deal with the conflict, a number of options may be considered:

1. Attempt to define and describe the conflict in cooperative terms (that is, as a common problem).

2. Try to deal with issues rather than personalities.

3. Deal with one issue at a time.

4. Focus on issues while they are small rather than permitting them to grow over time and become large ones.

5. Attempt to persuade one another rather than using threats, intimidation, and power plays.

6. Opt for full disclosure of all facts rather than allowing "hidden agendas" (leftover feelings or old arguments not settled) to function.

7. Encourage the validation of the other parties' interests or concerns. (Feelings are valid no matter what the facts are.)

8. Emphasize what you still hold in common.

9. Attempt to portray a trusting and friendly attitude.

10. Opt for a "win-win" resolution (a piece of the pie for everyone) rather than a "win-lose" result.

11. Attempt to generate as many new ideas and as much new information as possible in order to broaden the perspective of all persons involved.

12. Include all principal parties involved in the conflict at a common meeting.

13. Clarify whether you are dealing with one conflict or multiple conflicts.

14. Show basic respect for others, whether or not you agree with their ideas or positions.

Force Field Analysis

A helpful option is the use of a "force field analysis chart" to help a group determine the balance of forces moving toward a solution to the problem (driving forces) and the forces resisting a solution to the problem (restraining forces). Force field analysis was developed by the late Kurt Lewin, who is considered the father of social psychology in the United States. His idea was that within any group will be a combination of forces moving for a solution to a problem along with powerful forces resisting a solution. Interestingly, in some groups conflict erupts over the fact that some want to solve a problem while others fight against solving the problem, often for hidden reasons.

How to Use Force Field Analysis

In order to do a force field analysis, state the problem or conflict across the top of a piece of paper. Next, divide the paper in half and list all the driving forces on the left and all the restraining forces on the right, as shown on the next page.

Statement of Problem or Conflict Requiring a Solution[2]

Driving Forces (+)	Restraining Forces (-)
1.	1.
2.	2.
3.	3.
4.	4.
5.	5.
6.	6.
7.	7.
8.	8.
9.	9.
10.	10.

Next, go back and underline any forces, driving or restraining, that you deem most important right now. For each restraining force you underlined, attempt to formulate possible action steps that might reduce or eliminate its negative force against the driving forces. Sometimes brainstorming ideas for action is a quick and efficient way to generate many ideas for action steps.

Now go to the list of driving forces that you underlined and develop possible action steps that might increase and strengthen the force. Again, brainstorming ideas for action may be the quickest and most effective way to develop a maximum number of options for solution.

Review all the steps taken so far and evaluate them. Has anything been missed in haste? Is an action step only going to generate even more restraint from the other side of the field of forces? Determine all resources and leadership available and needed to implement the solution of the conflict.

The key idea behind force field analysis in dealing with conflict is to define the conflict as a problem held in common by all persons concerned and requiring a solution. It is important to note that a force field analysis may have more items on one side of the chart than the other. The positive and negative columns do not have to have the same number of items unless it just happens that way.

Let us take a typical local organizational problem and show how force field analysis could be applied to it. The problem requiring a solution would be stated as follows:

The Budget Needs to Be Cut by 25 Percent Next Year [3]

Forces Favoring a Cut (+)	Forces Against a Cut (-)
1. Income is down from last year.	1. Department staff favor this budget and know it is a favorite area with members of the organization.
2. There are fewer persons in the department.	2. An expansion of our department's programs/services is desired by the head of our total organization.
3. The department director is not as well trained as we desire.	3. Cuts in this area of our organization will have more ripple effects negatively than most would ever have.
	4. Items in other areas of the budget could be cut without harming our overall program so drastically.
	5. New members are attracted to our programs and services largely due to this department's area of work.
	6. The department head could be sent for more training to expand his/her competence on the job.

Having underlined the forces that seem most important right now, let us consider possible action steps to reduce forces one and four on the left side that favor a cut. First, income might be increased through a more vigorous financial canvass of the membership this year. Second, other large givers might be approached to underwrite the department's program to a larger degree. Third, a meeting could be arranged with the department members who want a separate budget in order to listen to their concerns and try to persuade them to work within regular budget channels. A similar process of action steps could be developed for the right side of the chart regarding the forces against a cut.

Next, review and evaluate all action steps developed so far. Choose action steps that seem most likely to work out and appoint leadership personnel to implement them.

Another option is to request the services of a trained outside consultant to work with the group, organization, or church in dealing with its conflict. Or it may be that the group has persons already trained in human relations skills and can call on their expertise as facilitators or consultants to help resolve the conflict.

The Values Crunch in Conflict Situations

A clash in values (strong beliefs and convictions) between persons and groups often serves as a trigger to conflict. Whereas the field of behavioral sciences places a positive value on constructive, creative conflict, religious and other voluntary organizations have placed a negative value on conflicts of almost any kind. By reexamining one's traditional religious value on conflict avoidance or conflict denial, the leader can be placed in an internal value conflict. Unless a leader can consciously place a positive value on conflict, he or she will tend to avoid, deny, rationalize, or overcontrol the conflict so as to resolve it prematurely. If a conflict is resolved prematurely (closed off, or superficial agreements reached), then the conflict will reappear ("recycle") at a later time. Conflict is cyclical in nature and will reappear predictably until the actual roots are dealt with and resolved. Consequently leader comfort with and valuing of constructive utilization of conflict in groups is a prerequisite for effective group leadership. Usually the first place to begin to get comfortable with conflict is to probe one's value system regarding conflict.

"Conflict utilization" is a new notion in the field of conflict studies. The phrase presupposes a positive value placed on a constructive use of conflict. (Clearly no one would value a destructive conflict.) *Utilization* is a dynamic word that is intended to mean that the energy involved in conflict be allowed to express itself in constructive ways ("utilized") rather than having a group hold in its strong conflictual feelings and depress itself.

It is the purpose of this chapter to challenge the reader to consider a deep reexamination of her or his value system regarding conflict. The average reader may discover a real difference between the values he or she has been raised with and a positive valuing of constructive conflict.

Chapter 5

Decision Making in Small Groups

The larger picture of small-group functioning begins to be sketched on the canvas of a religious or voluntary organization's culture, context, socio-economic milieu, and the actual purpose(s) of each small group. In religious, voluntary, and nonprofit organizations, decision making is constantly a challenge. Decisions need to be correct and supported enthusiastically by all involved in implementing them. The energy, commitment, loyalty, and vision of all members is needed for the decisions and actions to be successful. It is vital, then, that the underlying steps and psychology of *why and how decisions are made* be understood in such organizations. It is crucial that leadership personnel be given some training in this area especially. To this end this chapter seeks to summarize for the reader some of the most important research done on decision making, explain its basic steps, show where decisions can go wrong, and relate it to where one works with decisions.

Problems and challenges require decisions. The immediate problem needs a clear, brief, and understandable definition before proceeding further. The art of defining and clearly identifying the various parts of a problem or challenge is frequently short-circuited during a group's desire to accomplish a lot in too brief a time. Yes, "haste makes waste." Research indicates that when the stress and tension level gets too high or intense, the human mind has a tendency to begin to block out other alternatives and focus narrowly on just one. This is the area in which many groups overlook taking whatever time is *really* needed to describe and define adequately the problem that needs solving. In brief, it is quite possible to make a decision on *only a portion* of the overall problem and unknowingly assume that the whole thing is solved.

Values and Decision Making

If we believe that conflict is negative and to be avoided, we can develop *a blind spot in our perception and understanding of what is happening.* A blind spot can set us up for selective perceptions and hearing so we see and hear only that with which we are comfortable. From this basic stance we place ourselves in a position of desiring to hear only positive things or deciding only positive things pertaining to self, others, the group, or the organization. When feedback or data is *negative*, we begin to feel hurt or threatened. Is it any surprise that the negative value or belief assigned to conflict and dealing with differences in religious and voluntary organizations may have direct influence on decisions and how they are made?

We can rush through decision making, but we pay a price for it in more ways than we realize. The following are basic steps an individual takes in order to decide something.

Individual Decision Making: Action Steps

1. Define the problem and state it as specifically as possible.

2. Gather information necessary to analyze and prioritize all available choices.

3. Develop potential decisions and/or alternatives that correctly address the situation.

4. As objectively as possible, select the alternative with the best cost/benefit ratio.

5. Write out an action plan with alternatives.

6. Implement the action plan.

7. Monitor the action plan as it is carried out.

8. Evaluate the action plan and then replan for the next time it may occur and integrate what has been learned to date.

In contrast, let us now consider the steps a group experiences as it makes a decision.

Group Decision Making: Action Steps

1. Determine group roles, functions, responsibilities, and the common purpose.

2. Establish a climate in which ideas and feelings can be shared openly and comfortably.

3. State the problem, issue, or decision opportunity clearly.

4. Gather necessary information from all group members, since each member represents a resource center of information.

5. Analyze information and synthesize areas of agreement.

6. Consider the advantages and disadvantages of each decision alternative.

7. Select the most viable decision(s) by considering both positive and negative consequences.

8. Make an action plan that clearly identifies specific steps, responsibilities, reporting, and accountability network, and time frames by which each part of the plan should be done.

9. Implement the action plan.

10. Monitor and evaluate the action plan. Take learnings and integrate them into a revised action plan should this type of decision and action be required in the future.

Even as a small group makes a decision in a church or voluntary organization, it may unknowingly skip or rush a few steps and silently fall into an inferior or even defective decision. Some signs of a defective decision are described below.

Signs of Defective Decision Making

1. An incomplete survey of all the alternatives available.

2. An incomplete survey of all the objectives possible.

3. Failure to examine risks of preferred choice.

4. A poor or incomplete information and data search.

5. Using a selective bias in processing the information at hand.

6. Failure to reappraise initially rejected alternatives.

7. Failure to work out contingency plans.[1]

Group Think

When some of the preceding signs of defective decision making begin to occur, it is also possible that a small group or even a larger organization can begin to drift into what Dr. Janis calls "group think." Group think can be characterized by the following components, based on the original group think symptoms developed by Dr. Janis:

1. Individuals overestimate wisdom or accuracy of the group.

2. Individuals in the group begin to feel an illusion of invulnerability.

3. A climate of closed-mindedness to any outside information develops.

4. A series of collective rationalizations for the group's decision grows.

5. A stereotype of "out groups" (those outside of the group) emerges.

6. Pressure towards conformity for the anticipated group decision increases.

7. Self-censorship seeps in, and individuals remain silent even when they know the group decision is wrong or at least inferior. (In research this is often termed "dropping data.")

8. Next, the illusion of unanimity permeates the atmosphere.

9. If anyone tries to dissent or disagree, substantial pressure is directed at such individuals to conform or be silent.

10. Self-appointed "mind guards" (those who protect the group from adverse information) arise in the group.[2]

The following figure graphically shows how (1) antecedent conditions lead to symptoms of (2) "group think," which lead to (3) symptoms of defective decision making.[3]

Figure 3

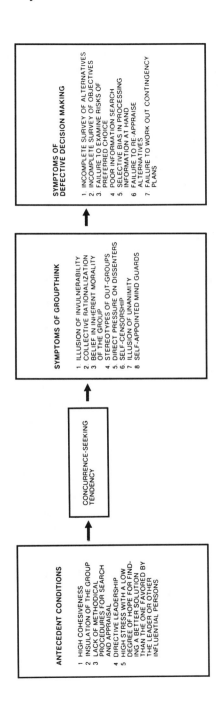

Typical illustrations of defective decision making and/or group hink are organizations pushing ahead to do fund raising, build buildings, add staff, and expand programs when there is a decline in membership and giving or changing demographics, which indicates less than unified support for expansion. Please note: it is fairly easy for a few to force or manipulate the larger membership into a decision, but there is little assurance in the long haul that those silent, disenfranchised members will readily work to support such a decision. So the question is, "What was gained and what was lost in rushing the decision?" Time will always tell.

In his earlier writings, Dr. Janis defined five stages in personal decision making. With each of the five stages, he indicated that key questions need to be raised by the decision maker as follows:[4]

Stages in Arriving at a Stable Decision

Stage	Key Question
1. Appraising the challenge.	1. Are the risks serious if I do not change?
2. Surveying the alternatives.	2. Is this alternative an acceptable means for dealing with the challenge? Have I sufficiently surveyed the available alternatives?
3. Weighing the alternatives.	3. Which alternative is best? Could the best alternative meet the essential needs?
4. Deliberating about commitment.	4. Shall I implement the best alternative and allow others to know?
5. Adhering despite negative feedback.	5. Are the risks serious if I do not change? Are the risks serious if I do change?

From his long-term research on decision making at Yale University, Dr. Janis developed the following form, which I have found useful with individuals and groups:[5]

Decision-making Balance Sheet

Decision to be made: _____

Expected consequences	Positive anticipations	Negative anticipations
Tangible gains and losses for self	1.	1.
	2.	2.
	3.	3.
Tangible gains and losses for others	1.	1.
	2.	2.
	3.	3.
Self-approval or self-disapproval	1.	1.
	2.	2.
	3.	3.
Social approval or disapproval	1.	1.
	2.	2.
	3.	3.

How to Use This Balance Sheet

Before beginning the process, the individual or group should articulate the pending decision and write it on the blank line at the top of the page.

First, the group is supposed to think through the expected consequences in both a positive as well as a negative way for the four different gains and losses as well as in the areas of self-approval and social approval vs. disapproval. Second, mentally weigh and evaluate the positive and negative anticipations in all four areas shown in the left column. Third, the exercise of weighing anticipated consequences can act as a "mental balance sheet" of pluses and minuses as the group formulates a decision. This process of weighing and evaluating all the pluses and minuses may take time. It is worth the time invested!

Decisional Conflict

Decisions typically involve us in some degree of confusion, ambivalence, and turmoil, if not mental and emotional conflict. Our questions range from "what should I do?" and "what is the best decision out of all these possibilities?" to "what if I make a mistake and fail to make a perfect decision when so many people are counting on me?" and "how can I best sort out this mess of details and information before I finalize a decision?"

Janis and Mann developed the concept of "decisional conflict" to describe a scenario wherein the individual feels pulled in opposite directions at the same time ("Should I join this organization or should I not join?"). Typical signs of decisional conflict include hesitation, vacillation, feelings of uncertainty, or acute signs of stress. A common trigger for this stress is the fear of risking a major loss or reversal if the incorrect decision is made. Another common dynamic is the feeling of being in a double bind, that is, whichever way I decide, I will lose or be wrong.

The following five feelings (stages) were developed by Janis and Mann to demonstrate the series of interrelated feelings and thoughts a person or group may experience during decisional conflict:[6]

1. *Unconflicted Inertia:* This is the stage in which a person does not feel any significant level of stress or pressure and does not anticipate any major loss if a decision is made. In brief, there is no immediate pressure to make a decision. Decisions are mainly contemplated. Yet, the danger here can be a tendency to procrastinate, to put off a decision for too long!

2. *Unconflicted Change:* In this stage a person or group begins to realize that a new course of action is necessary and something needs to be decided and acted upon. Feeling that change to a new course of action or direction will present no major risk(s) (such as a loss of membership, budget, or power), the person or group decides to move ahead and make a decision. Although some serious risks may be involved, the risks are not clearly perceived. Unconflicted change can lead to a series of small incremental changes (decisions) that are consecutive and progressive yet seem small within themselves. The danger is that all these seemingly small decisions are not surveyed or evaluated in an overall manner to provide the bigger picture with its longer-range implications. When all the options are not evaluated as each decision is implemented, a defective decision may surface later on when seen with hindsight.

3. *Defensive Avoidance:* During this stage of decision making, one tries to prevent any form of communication that might expose the deficiencies or weaknesses in the decisions or actions taken or anticipated. Unless the person/group avoids new information or questioning that challenges the decision about to be made, the person/group will be plunged into emotional conflict/confusion about the anticipated decision (or one made recently). For this reason people try to avoid others they suspect will challenge or disapprove of their decision. For the same reason persons very close to us are often the last to be informed since we know them well enough to know what they will say to challenge us or disapprove of our decision. We do not want anyone to disapprove or question our decision once it is made. We want closure and a feeling that "it is done." It is psychologically painful to question a decision once made and acted on.

4. *Hypervigilance:* By this stage people can be under such severe stress that they suffer serious errors in judgment, cognitive

constriction (overly focused on one idea or option), high levels of vacillation, and even the repetition of the same thought over and over. Hypervigilant persons/groups tend to make snap judgments and take quick, drastic actions that are ill-advised and frequently mistakes. (It is possible that "pilot error" or "air traffic control tower error" in airline accident investigations are actually scenarios in which key persons were experiencing hypervigilance and did not realize that their high level of stress set them up for a fatal decision.)

5. *Vigilance:* Once the individual/group has moved through the hypervigilance stage and avoided making any rash decisions despite the very high level of stress and tension, they are more relaxed and stable, with only moderate stress remaining. By this time one begins to feel that a better answer may be discovered, and adequate time is devoted to a more careful search for and evaluation of alternative solutions. A more focused search pattern for new data is used to allow for a more precise appraisal of all alternatives prior to a final decision.

Immediate decisional options are carefully weighed against longer-term decisions that may require more time and thus delay an immediate decision. The need to reduce stress in the small-group decision-making process may prompt a quick decision in order to say "we are done!" Rash decisions can lead to serious mistakes by short-circuiting the normal process of examining all possible alternatives prior to the final decision time. Groups can easily overlook the subtle process so that we can say yes to a decision to either (1) avoid verbal conflict with others or (2) simply "please" the leader. The real test for a decision made is whether all who said yes will work hard to make it happen and support it in the light of future opposition.

It is important for the reader to know that it is typical of both individual and/or group decision making to vacillate when making a decision. The vacillation process can cause a confusing type of regression from "defensive avoidance" back to "unconflicted inertia" and then begin the process all over again through the five stages. It is possible to move as far as the "hypervigilance" stage and then regress to one of the three earlier stages and start over again. It is important to know that this type of recycling back and forth amongst the various stages is normative in decision making and does not mean anything is wrong with either the individual or the group. One way to describe it is a series of dress rehearsals before the real decision is ready for opening night.

Since stress is an expected and common part of the decision-making process, let us review some ideas on managing our stress.

Stress Management

Few things can become more stressful than making a decision. When we mix the normative stresses of decision making with the additional stresses common to small-group dynamics, we have a strong mixture of stressors. What are some of the best ways to manage our stress?

Some authorities simply define *stress* as "anything that places an extra demand on you."[7] Others define it as anything we cannot control but where we want or need control. Perhaps the most famous definition of stress was given by Dr. Hans Selye, who wrote that "stress is the nonspecific response of the body to any demand made upon it." Stress impacts us physically, emotionally, and mentally—totally. Experts agree that a certain percentage of stress is normal and good for us. Yet, too much of a good thing can turn negative and have serious influences on our total functioning, including our decision making.

Three Ways to Cope with Stress

Three standard ways to increase your capacity to cope with stress are:[8]

1. Reduce the quantity and/or difficulty of the tasks that confront you.

2. Reduce the time pressure you are under to complete the tasks.

3. Increase your coping skills through reeducation.

The Relaxation Response

One of the best known authorities on relaxation is Dr. Herbert Benson, who wrote about the relaxation response. He suggested four steps to help us relax and manage our stress level:[9]

1. Select a quiet place. Not too noisy. Sit upright and get in a comfortable position. Breathe deeply and slowly!

2. Select a word or phrase or even compose a brief prayer. Just repeat the word, phrase, or prayer over and over to yourself either silently or very softly depending on where you are located.

3. Adopt a passive attitude. Let things happen. Don't resist anything. Just keep repeating what you were saying in No. 2.

4. Close your eyes, but do not fall asleep.

Ten Ways to Manage/Reduce Stress

Additional activities you can use or explore for your own personal stress management program may include one or more of the following:

1. Relaxation training
2. Biofeedback training
3. Physical exercise
4. Rational-thinking training/reading
5. Problem-solving techniques
6. Role playing
7. Assertiveness training/reading
8. Breathing exercises
9. Communications training
10. Prayer, meditation, and imaging

Chapter 6

Change, Systems, and Paradoxes

Change

Change is sweeping the world like a strong prevailing wind. It blows on everyone and everything in its path! It makes no exceptions and grants no immunity to individuals, organizations, or even nations. It is everywhere.

Innovation has been described by various experts as the process by which new ideas or solutions are introduced into human systems and organizations to improve the status quo.

Change Defined

One of the best definitions of *change* comes from Webster's New Collegiate Dictionary, which indicates that *change* means "to make something different, to replace with another, to shift or change direction, to exchange or to experience a transition or transformation."

In concert with the preceding definition and building on it, Dr. Rosabeth Moss Kanter, management consultant, writes that change

> involves the crystallization of new action possibilities (new policies, new behaviors, new patterns, new methodologies . . .) based on reconceptualized patterns in the organization. The architecture of change involves the design and construction of new patterns, or the reconceptualization of old ones, to make new, and hopefully more productive, actions possible.

Organizations that are change-oriented, then, will have a large
number of integrative mechanisms encouraging fluidity of
boundaries, the free flow of ideas, and the empowerment of
people to act on new information.[1]

Given the pervasiveness of change, it is important to take a brief
look at the importance of organizational culture to better understand
the overall context and variables that influence an organization and
all the small groups that are part of it.

In contrast to those who welcome or encourage change, there are
a few who resist change. Dr. Kanter named this antichange orientation "segmentalism." These people tend to compartmentalize
things into separate entities and fail to see the whole picture. As Dr.
Kanter indicates, "segmentalist approaches see problems as narrowly as possible, independently of their context, independently of
their connections to any other problems."[2]

Organizational Culture

The organizational culture of a small group in a church or
voluntary organization is the milieu in which the groups exist
and from which it derives its character and purpose(s). Various
experts define *culture* as a pattern of basic assumptions, values,
beliefs, philosophy, feelings/climate, and expected behaviors
commonly held and practiced by the members of the organization. It is quite common for a larger organization to have multiple
subcultures that comprise the larger culture of the total organizational system. It is difficult to understand a group or organizational culture without first comprehending its basic assumptions
and beliefs. Culture commonly has three levels or dimensions:
(1) *artifacts and creations* (technology, art, visible behavior
patterns), (2) *values* (tested by social consensus), and (3) *basic
assumptions* (about environment, reality, human nature, activity,
and human relationships).[3] By understanding an organization's
culture, it is easier to comprehend the organizational system
dynamics.

Systems

Organizational Systems

Organizations are living systems. They are comprised of people, organizational structure (which includes small groups, boards, and committees; power and control issues; vested interests; financial issues; moral and ethical issues; ways of thinking and believing), and a series of checks and balances that lend themselves to a sense of equilibrium or imbalance, as the case may be.

In *The Fifth Discipline* Dr. Peter Senge, of the Massachusetts Institute of Technology, indicates that

> systems thinking is a discipline for seeing wholes. It is a framework for seeing interrelationships rather than things, for seeing patterns of change rather than static "snapshots".... The essence of the discipline of systems thinking lies in a shift of mind: seeing interrelationships rather than linear cause-effect chains, and seeing processes of change rather than snapshots.[4]

He continues his writing about feedback by noting that there are two types of feedback in a system: (1) *reinforcing feedback* processes and (2) *balancing feedback (or stabilizing)* processes. In the reinforcing feedback type, a small change can build upon itself, producing continued movement in the original direction. Sometimes this type of feedback starts off negatively and only continues to worsen. That is called a "vicious cycle." Cycles that begin in a positive manner are often termed "virtuous cycles." In the balancing type of feedback, the system is seeking stability. A balancing system has a way to be self-correcting as needed.[5]

Systems and Leaders

From a systems perspective, the real task of a leader is "designing the learning processes whereby people throughout the organization can deal productively with the critical issues they face . . ."[6] The systems perspective on leadership and leader development is antithetical to the usual philosophy of leadership development in our culture, which is the leader telling others what to do! When training small-group leaders, it is important to be clear on which type of culture and organizational system one is training them for and which specific type of leadership style and skills one expects them to know and practice.

A systems perspective requires more time than a leader-dominated one. Some organizations are impatient and want results now—or yesterday! Impatience can breed short-term answers and premature solutions that do not lead to permanent, long-term answers. It all depends on the goals, beliefs, philosophy, values, and expectations of the organization. What kinds of small groups does it desire and what type of small-group leaders does it desire to develop and train? These are more serious questions to address than most religious and voluntary organizations are willing to allow time for. A compelling exercise would be for an organization to write a five-page paper on its organizational philosophy or theology and its basic values as a foundation prior to developing any small-group leaders. What are we developing or training leadership for and specifically what do we expect them to do?

Now, in light of pervasive change and our knowledge of organizational culture and systems, let us conclude with a brief examination of the paradox of many small-group leaders; that is, we are expected to provide stability while simultaneously dealing with constant change.

Paradox

One of the most confusing areas in religion as well as many voluntary organizations is that of paradox. A paradox is simply the coexistence of two things or statements that apparently contradict one another, often simultaneously. Paradoxical opposites we frequently encounter on a regular basis include:

love—hate
good—bad
sacred—secular
stability—change
peace—war
acceptance—rejection

certainty—doubt
belief—disbelief
hope—hopelessness

Leaders in voluntary and/or religious organizations (lay and professional) are often caught in confusing paradoxical situations. Most leaders try to work with or solve one side of the paradox and ignore or deny the other side. In churches a typical example would be to modernize their place of worship while still retaining some traditional rituals and symbols important to them. In voluntary organizations it might be how to develop new membership recruitment procedures without eliminating older procedures that have helped attract new members over the years.

The best strategy is to acknowledge and understand that both sides of the paradox are functioning simultaneously, and the real answer may be found in working with the *reciprocal process* of the situation, moving from one side back to the other side of the paradox ad infinitum. Interventions into the reciprocal *process* may be more effective than only dealing with the *content* on one side of the paradox. In brief, the key is to see the paradox as a dynamic reciprocal process as opposed to only two fixed yet opposite positions or entities.

The climate and culture of church, religious institutions, and voluntary organizations is rapidly changing. Formerly most authority figures were respected, accepted, and largely unchallenged. Today the opposite is happening. Authority figures in most major professions are less respected and more open to questions, challenges, and criticisms than ever before. Culture and attitudes are changing! People seem to question and challenge everyone and everything. This questioning/challenging process is pervasive and need not be personalized by any professional or lay leader in an organization.

Clergy as well as lay leaders in religious or voluntary organizations need to understand the reciprocal process, which shifts from some respect and trust in them over to direct questioning and challenging of their leadership and authority and then recycles again and again. Consider the fact that churches as well as voluntary organizations (such as PTAs, Girl and Boy Scouts, and YMCAs and YWCAs) are the only social institutions left in our culture where people can question and challenge authority figures and not get fired for it. Perhaps that is one of our greatest challenges in the future: How do we reach out to those with such personal needs and still keep them in our organizations and small groups in a helpful way?

Outreach

There is a major need to reach out to persons with special needs. The list of those in need seems endless; only a few are mentioned here as examples. It is largely churches, religious institutions, volunteer organizations (including food banks, Habitat for Humanity, homeless shelters, the Salvation Army, and so on) who provide outreach to those in need over and above the local, state, or federal programs. But if any of the persons with special needs are mentally ill or emotionally different, our organizations are largely untrained and uncomfortable in reaching out to them.

I suggest that churches, religious organizations, and voluntary organizations begin to envision new forms of training so that their small-group leaders can meet these special needs. There are needs for community-supported therapy groups, guidance or rehabilitation groups, career counseling groups, parent education groups, children and youth support groups after school for latchkey children or those whose parents are separated or divorced. Some of these areas cited above require highly trained professional therapists and/or group facilitators. More and more professionals are doing pro bono work at either no fee or offering very low discounted fees to service some of the above populations. It is worth asking professionals to lend your organization a hand to provide training in your community. They can be either a free or low-fee source of professional training for some of the small-group facilitators your organization needs!

Leading a small group of any kind is one of the most interesting things a person can ever do. Group facilitation can be fun and challenging. It is more complex than most expect. It is a system of people interacting in varied ways and on multiple levels simultaneously. Where could one find more challenges?

The paradox is that we all want challenges and yet don't want challenges all at the same time.

Additional Resources

At the end of this book is a series of small-group leader/facilitator training workshops for those who desire some initial ideas in how to organize such training within their organization. In addition, I've included a collection of resources—selected charts and handout materials—to add to the practical value of the book. A bibliography is also included for those desiring to do further reading.

Chapter 7

Training Workshops for Small-Group Leaders

Thus far, background material has been presented for the reader to understand the context, stages of development, and leadership styles of groups. We will now focus attention on a series of two-hour small-group training workshops for use in local church or voluntary organization settings.

The workshops will cover the following areas:
1. Decision Making
2. Task and Maintenance Functions
3. Leadership Styles and Interventions
4. Conflict in Values
5. Resistance and How to Cope with It
6. Creative Conflict-Resolution Techniques

Rationale for Workshops

These workshop outlines are included in the book because of the assumption that we learn best through experience. It is important for the reader to reflect on how she or he best learns. Is it only through reading that we learn a skill or sport? Or is it through repeated experience and practice?

Based on the belief that we learn best through experience, this chapter is designed so that the workshop leader and participants may learn from one another through the brief experiences outlined herein or through some form of adaptation of these workshop ideas.

Each of the workshops may be held separately or as a series of two or more. This book is to be used as a resource for background and guidance by the church or other voluntary organization conducting the workshops. Each session is completely outlined within this chapter as an aid to the leader. After carefully planning for each session, the leader will conduct the session for the group members. A leader may or may not be a member of the organization desiring the training. Sometimes an outside trainer/facilitator can be more effective than someone who is "just another member" to those inside the organization.

Instructions to Workshop Leaders

Leader Preparation

Each workshop leader is asked to read this entire book as background for the workshop. Page references to key portions of the book for additional background reading are given in the workshop instructions. Background material with key ideas for the workshop participants to read and think about can be written on newsprint or chalkboard. (Certainly, every workshop participant would be best prepared if he or she purchased and read this entire book as preparation, but you will have to determine what is most workable for your situation.) Finally, workshop leaders may desire to read some of the additional books listed in the bibliography. Leaders may duplicate copies of any forms or charts in this book for use in their workshop sessions.

Workshop Times

The suggested amounts of time for each portion of each workshop are only approximations. In some cases, the time may be just right. In other instances, leaders may need to lengthen the time if workshop participants desire more time for discussion of the topic involved. In brief, *be flexible in adjusting workshop times as needed.*

Size of Groups

The suggested number of twelve persons in a workshop is only intended as an average size. Obviously, you may have fewer or more than twelve in a given workshop. Here are some suggestions for making each workshop flexible, regardless of the number of persons who attend.

If you have more than twelve persons, you may assign a few more to the role of observer. If you have twenty-four persons, you can run two simultaneous workshops by giving each group the same instructions. Then you can move from one group to another and give them guidance. Or you can arrange for a second person to work with the second group of twelve.

If you have fewer than twelve persons participating, perhaps only six to eight, you may decide to postpone the workshop until you can secure twelve or more persons. You may decide to combine your workshop with that of another nearby church or voluntary organization and share leadership with them. Or you may decide to proceed with the workshop, using whatever number you have. For example, a group of seven persons could be arranged as follows for Workshop 1: a group of four could be designated the committee to decide on teaching time. The other three persons could be given combined observer assignments with one person observing for questions 1 and 2, a second person observing for questions 3 and 4, and a third person observing for question 5.

Each subsequent workshop in this chapter may be conducted with fewer than twelve persons by simply allocating fewer persons to each assignment and by combining assignments to each person or by eliminating certain questions or assignments if they do not appear practical for your organization.

Physical Arrangements

Physically arranging the room is an important part of the workshop leader's responsibilities. You should personally check the room for adequate heating or cooling, lighting, seating for number expected (circles are an ideal arrangement), paper/pencil supplies, newsprint, markers, crayons, tape, tacks, scissors, chalk and chalkboards, and name tags for everyone. Coffee, tea, and snacks may be desired also.

Getting Acquainted

It is assumed that most persons attending a local church or voluntary organization workshop will know one another already. If so, please feel free to minimize time needed to help persons get acquainted. However, if all persons do not know one another, workshop leaders may desire to include an additional thirty minutes for getting-acquainted time.

Having persons talk in twos about their favorite vacation places, the most exciting times they have ever had, what they like most about their group/organization, and background on their families or jobs are usually winners for helping people get acquainted. Another option is to have persons talk in twos for ten minutes and then take one minute to introduce that person to the total group and vice versa.

Leader discretion will be needed in deciding whether or not getting-acquainted time is needed. If so, be sure to include the necessary time in the estimated workshop schedule for this important process. The time to "break the ice" and get acquainted is *not* a waste of time. It is sometimes the most important "maintenance function" to be done to assure a smooth and comfortable flow for the workshop.

Leader Options

Additional leader options for any of the workshops may include using a role-play instead of any of the discussion suggested. Or a leader may desire to have part of an actual church board or voluntary group committee meeting tape-recorded (with permission, of course) and play an actual segment for the workshop session to analyze in light of the questions posed in each workshop topic area. Another option would be for the leader personally to write up a brief case study of a board or committee discussion for workshop participants to study and analyze. Or, the leader might ask a member of a board or committee to write up such a segment of a meeting and share it in the workshop.

Workshop Observers

It is important for the workshop leader to type and duplicate copies of all instructions and questions for the observers in each workshop. Instructions and questions are contained within each workshop description in this chapter. Specifically, the main assignment to communicate to observers is that they are to watch for and record in writing samples any statements they hear related to the specific question assigned to them.

Workshop Final Discussion

During the final discussion time in each of the workshops, the leader will want to guide the group in asking: (1) How has this experience been helpful to me personally? (2) How has this experience been helpful to my board, committee, or group? (3) How will this experience be helpful to my church or voluntary organization?

Workshop 1

Decision Making

An effective decision involves the following characteristics:

1. A clear definition of the issue about which the group needs to make a decision;

2. A willingness of the group to state and work through major questions and reservations about the decision before it is made, carefully analyzing the blocks to the decision during the process of making it;

3. A consideration of a variety of alternatives and selection of the best alternative, with plans for implementation;

4. A utilization of the resources (such as knowledge and skills) of the group members;

5. An acceptance of the decision by the group with a willingness to support and carry out the decision;

6. An assignment of an expected time for the implementation of the decision along with the assignment of who will be responsible;

7. An agreement on an evaluation process.

Common causes of blocks to effective decision making include:

1. Past history of the group that involves unresolved issues and feelings;

2. A struggle for leadership and power among group members and between group members and the leader;

3. Fear of the implications and consequences of the decision;

4. Inappropriate methods of decision making for the particular situation (being dictatorial when people were expecting a democratic method);

5. Assumptions and expectations that are not checked out;

6. Inattention to group resistance, conflict, doubt, and questions.

Leader Assignment

For this workshop the leader will want to read chapters one through five of this book carefully. Duplicate copies of Form 1, entitled "Checklist on Decision Making," for all participants. Form 2, entitled "Checklist of Participants' and Leader's Responsibilities in Group Discussion," may be duplicated for members of Workshop 1. Form 2 may also be used as a general background resource for members of all workshops if so desired.

Outline for Workshop on Decision Making
(two hours)

Purpose:

To discover through practice what facilitates or hinders effective decision making.

Step 1 (thirty minutes):

Ask a maximum of seven people to work as a committee. The decision to be made is whether or not to lengthen the church-school teaching time by forty-five minutes per week. For a voluntary group it might be whether to begin a new series of programs or services. If another type of decision is more relevant to your group, substitute it.

Ask the remaining persons to observe the discussion in these five specific ways: (1) What seems to facilitate the group making the decision? (2) What seems to block the group from making the decision? (3) What types of questions are asked? (4) What feelings are expressed (like anger, frustration, doubt, confidence, and so on)? and (5) Who speaks to whom? Each of the five observers should take careful notes of actual behaviors, including specific quotes or instances of behavior observed.

It will be helpful if the leader writes these five questions on chalkboard or newsprint or has a copy for each observer.

Step 2 (twenty-five minutes):

Have each of the observers share her or his observations with the group of seven for a maximum of five minutes per observer.

Step 3 (fifteen minutes):

Ask the group to resume the original discussion in light of the observer feedback just heard. The task is to try to reach a decision by incorporating the feedback just received.

Step 4 (twenty minutes):

Each of the observers shares a second round of observations for only four minutes per observer with the group.

Step 5 (twenty-five minutes):

The total group has a general discussion regarding what has been observed and learned about effective decision making in a group. (See the characteristics of effective decision making listed at the opening of this workshop.)

Give participants copies of Form 1, "Checklist on Decision Making." Suggest that individuals rate themselves. Then in triads (groups of three) individuals can check their perception of themselves with how the other two people see them.

If more time is desired, a group could agree to meet a second time on another date, repeat the above process, and attempt to go further by selecting another type of problem it needs to make a decision about and use the observer feedback process as suggested.

Step 6 (five minutes):

The leader may wish to share with the group the information on decision making found at the beginning of this workshop.

Form 1

Checklist on Decision Making

The decisions you make for your own personal needs are important to you. Treat them with care by using the same methods social scientists recommend for group decision making.

Personal Checklist

In my decision processes I follow the procedure of:	Most of the time	Some of the time	Need to improve
1. Analyzing the problem in terms of all possible factors . . .			
2. Determining what my own motives are in recommending (or fighting) a change . . .			
3. Identifying (where possible) the feelings of others involved . . .			
4. Gathering as much objective information as I can before evaluating . . .			
5. Looking at my own skills of perception and analysis . . .			
6. Creating an atmosphere where others can differ from me . . .			
7. Checking during the implementation stage with a readiness to revise the original decision . . .			

Form 2

Checklist of Participants' and Leader's Responsibilities in Group Discussion

Preparation

A. Group Participants

1. Prepare to discuss.
2. Arrive on time.

B. Leader

1. Arranges for physical setting.

   —chairs and tables for all (no second-row seats)

   —temperature and lighting

   —chalkboard, chalk, and eraser, or newsprint, easel, and marker

   —name cards and crayons, if necessary

2. Prepares tentative outline.
3. Prepares some questions in advance of meeting.

   —to get discussion started

   —to keep discussion going purposefully

   —to help keep discussion related to experience of participants

   —to bring out all sides of topic

Discussion

A. Leader

1. Begins on time.
2. Introduces the topic.

   —suggests purpose of discussion

   —presents tentative outline

   —allows time for participants to adjust outline if necessary

3. Records participants' thoughts concisely on chalkboard or chart pad.
4. Erases contributions, with permission.

5. Draws all participants into discussion as soon as possible.

6. Helps people communicate when necessary.

7. Guides group to minimize useless speculation.

8. Gives "thought-flow" summaries when needed (repetition domination, clarification).

9. Keeps discussion on track (if desirable).

10. Remains neutral.

11. Does not become the center of attention by making speeches, standing unnecessarily, encouraging teacher-pupil or leader-participant atmosphere, commenting on each contribution, or sitting apart from the group.

B. Group Participants

1. Help adjust leader's outline.

2. Make contributions in the language of the group.

3. Bring out all sides of the question.

4. Accept and support each other as unique individuals.

5. Try to prevent domination of the discussion.

6. Help each other understand what is said.

7. Add to one another's contributions spontaneously.

8. Build upon others' contributions (avoid leaving contributions dangling).

9. Listen actively.

10. Help keep discussion on the track.

11. Draw other participants into the discussion.

Closing

A. Leader

1. Stops discussion on time or before interest wanes.

2. Presents final summary of consensus and of differing opinions.

B. Group Participants

1. Adjust leader's summary (if necessary).

2. Plan next meeting: leader, topic, materials to study, date.

Workshop 2

Task and Maintenance Functions

Groups usually assemble for a purpose. An immediate task of a group is to define its purpose and clarify for all present why everyone is there. The task of a group is normally the stated business or purpose (task) for which persons have agreed to meet and work together.

Task functions that enable a group to function effectively were described in Chapter 1. These task functions are to:

1. *Initiate—suggest new ideas, methods, or solutions in order to enable the group to fulfill its task.*

2. *Clarify—ask questions or make statements that assist the group to move toward its goal(s). It can mean checking out assumptions and expectations that have not been shared up to a given point in the discussion.*

3. *Analyze—divide broader issues and problems into smaller, more workable steps for discussion and solution.*

4. *Summarize*—pull together the loose ends. A summary statement enables a group to realize where it is and how much it has accomplished.

5. *Seek Information and Opinions*—seek additional information or opinions in order to clarify values and opinions previously stated within the group.

Within a group, members have many feelings and needs, yet seldom are these expressed in a work group or committee meeting. In order for a group to function smoothly and effectively, a healthy emotional climate needs to be maintained and attended to: hence, the term *maintenance function.*

Maintenance functions within a group may include the following functions, which do get interwoven with the ongoing *task* functions on the basis of group need. These functions were described in chapter 1:

1. *Keep the Gate*—keep communication open and flowing, facilitating the flow of conversation, seeing that all persons have an opportunity to speak or to support a minority viewpoint.

2. *Encourage*--express warmth and responsiveness to other group members. It also means building upon other's ideas.

3. *Listen*—listen actively to the group conversation without participating in or attending to other distractions or fringe talk.

4. *Harmonize*--reconcile differences, relieve tension, and diplomatically explore reasons for differences.

5. *Set Standards*--suggest standards for group use in selecting content or methods. It may also include suggesting that the group evaluate its decisions or processes.

It is important to note that typical nonfunctional group roles may include blocking, aggressiveness, status seeking, dominating, hidden agendas, and special-interest persons pushing only one area of "pet" interest.

Leader Assignment

Read chapters 1 and 3. Duplicate Form 3, entitled "How I Perceived the Person."

Outline for Workshop on Task and Maintenance Functions (two hours)

Purpose:
To discover through practice how the use of the task and maintenance functions helps a group and how they are interrelated.

Step 1 (thirty minutes):
Divide the total group into a discussion group with at least three persons serving as observers. If the group is too large for a good discussion (more than seven to nine people), have more persons take the role of observers. Have the persons who are to be the discussion group select a task or a maintenance role that they will practice by pulling out of a box slips of paper on which a role has been written. One of the slips of paper will indicate that the person is to play a nonfunctional negative or blocking role.

The observers will each observe only one type of role—task, maintenance, or blocking. The observers are asked to keep actual quotes of what was said and what happened during the discussion. Form 3 may be used here.

Step 2 (fifteen minutes):

Each observer shares his or her observations for a maximum of five minutes each with the group.

Step 3 (fifteen minutes):

The discussion group responds to the three observers' feedback for fifteen minutes more by playing the roles a second time more effectively or asking questions about the task or maintenance role.

Step 4 (thirty minutes):

A general discussion of the importance of and problems with task and maintenance functions, as the group sees them, in the ongoing work of their group or organization.

Step 5 (fifteen minutes):

Each of the observers again provides a maximum of five minutes of feedback from their observations of the discussion in Step 4.

Step 6 (fifteen minutes):

The total group has a general discussion about task and maintenance functions, summarizing what they have learned about them during this workshop. Members may be encouraged to identify roles they will wish to put into practice in boards, committees, or program meetings as well as study groups they are in. The leader of the workshop gives additional input from chapter 1 of this book.

Form 3

How I Perceived the Person

Task-Maintenance Functions	Comments:	Group-Maintenance Functions	Comments:
1. Initiating: Proposing tasks or goals, defining a group problem, suggesting a procedure or ideas for solving a problem.		1. Encouraging: Being friendly, warm, and responsive to others; accepting others and their contributions; regarding others by giving them an opportunity for recognition.	
2. Information or opinion seeking: Requesting facts, seeking relevant information about a group concern, asking for suggestions and ideas.		2. Expressing group feelings: Sensing feeling, mood, relationships within the group; sharing own feeling or affect wih other member.	
3. Information or opinion giving: Offering facts, providing relevant information about group concern, stating a belief, giving suggestions or ideas.		3. Harmonizing: Attempting to reconcile disagreements, reducing tensions through "pouring oil on troubled waters," getting people to explore their differences.	
4. Clarifying or elaborating: Interpreting or reflecting ideas and suggestions, clearing up confusions, indicating alternatives and issues before the group, giving examples.		4. Compromising: When own idea or status is involved in a conflict, offering to compromise own position; admitting error, disciplining self to maintain group cohesion.	
5. Summarizing: Pulling together related ideas, restating suggestions after group has discussed them, offering a decision or conclusion for the group to accept or reject.		5. Gate-keeping: Attempting to keep communication channels open, facilitating the participation of others, suggesting procedures for sharing opportunity to discuss group problems.	
6. Consensus testing: Sending up trial balloons to see if group is nearing a conclusion, checking with group to see how agreement has been reached.		6. Setting standards: Expressing standards for group to achieve, applying standards in evaluating group function and production.	

Workshop 3

Leadership Styles and Interventions

For the purpose of this workshop, let us define *leadership* as a series of functions, including task and maintenance functions, that members are to provide, required for a group to function effectively and reach its goals. Clearly, then, leadership is a function that can be provided by one person, by several persons within a group, or by each person in the group. Ideally, in church and voluntary organizational groups, leadership is a series of functions provided by many persons involved in the group, including the designated leader. The more widely leadership functions are shared, the broader the base of group responsibility developed among the members. As was said in chapter 3, the functional theory of leadership presumes that leadership is an acquired set of skills that almost anyone can learn, given a few minimal basic skills within that person (like an ability to communicate clearly and an ability to assert oneself).

Leadership interventions are any questions, statements, emotions, selected silences, or changes in leadership style that influence a group to move toward its goal(s). Hence, any person within the group may make a leadership intervention into the group process.

Leader Assignment

Read chapter 3 carefully. Duplicate copies of the diagram "Leadership Behavior in Making Decisions" in chapter 3 and "Some Suggestions to Members of Discussion Groups," which is Form 4 in this chapter. These copies of Form 4 may be distributed in the workshop.

Outline for Workshop on Leadership Styles and Interventions (two hours)

Purpose:

To discover through practice what different leadership styles and interventions can do to a group.

Step 1 (thirty-five minutes):

In advance of the workshop, the leader asks three persons to volunteer or selects three persons to help with the workshop. Each of these persons is to demonstrate a different style of leadership with the group: *autocratic, democratic, laissez-faire.* (If necessary, the leader of the workshop could demonstrate all three styles.)

Give each person a written description of the style you wish her or him to demonstrate. Also make some suggestions about the kind of situation in which the demonstration is to take place: for example, the chairperson of a board or committee of a voluntary organization (select a specific one) or a church school teacher leading a class session. The autocratic teacher has prepared a lesson and is determined to teach it regardless of what the members of the class may desire. Or, the autocratic board/committee chairperson may or may not ask peoples' opinions but makes all the final decisions. The democratic leader encourages all to speak on the issues, plans for action from the suggestions, attempts to get consensus rather than a vote on an issue. As a church school teacher, the democratic leader encourages all viewpoints to be expressed. The laissez-faire leader may come into the group asking, "What do you want to do today?" and then sit and wait for the group to take responsibility.

Before each demonstration, the leader describes the situation, and members are asked to role-play the situation with the appointed person acting as leader.

Step 2 (fifteen minutes):

After the demonstrations, members of the group share how they feel about the different styles demonstrated. Use the following guidelines: (1) identify the leadership styles demonstrated; (2) express feelings about the leadership styles (what was going on inside of the persons during each demonstration); (3) identify what happens to a group when the different styles of leadership are used. For instance, what are the coping patterns of the members (fight, flight, denial, and so forth)?

Step 3 (ten minutes):

Divide the group into groups of three. Ask one group to discuss what they like or don't like about the autocratic leadership style and suggest when this style might be appropriate. Similarly, have a second group discuss the pros and cons of a laissez-faire leadership style. When is this style appropriate? Ask a third group to deal similarly with the democratic style. If you have more than nine people, groups of three could work on the same leadership style.

Step 4 (ten minutes):

Each group will share with the total group a summary of its discussion.

Step 5 (twenty minutes):

The total group will have a discussion regarding what the different styles and interventions can do to a group. The discussion may be partially focused on where the different leadership styles may be helpful within the life of a group or organization. The diagram on leadership behavior in chapter 3 may help to facilitate this discussion. Copies of this can be distributed to each member.

Step 6 (thirty minutes):

Take the group through the "Twenty Verbs Exercise" of chapter 3. The list of words can be put on newsprint or chalkboard, with persons writing their own lists or given a copy of the list.

Form 4

Some Suggestions
to Members of Discussion Groups

1. Come prepared to take responsibility for making a good discussion group, to share ideas, questions, and information as well as to listen. Too many quiet persons and few verbal participants make a group dull. If you have come along "just for the ride" or just "to see what is going on," you will profit more as a *participant* observer who experiences what is going on.

2. Be seated so you can see the faces of every other member of the group. Or rearrange the seats so you can see all faces. Avoid back rows and hidden locations.

3. Wear your name tag until you and others can call everyone by his or her name and practice using the names of others in the discussion.

4. Talk briefly and to the point. Stay on the topic. Avoid speeches. Don't take over the floor and keep it. No filibusters or long personal reminiscences, please.

5. After you have spoken, pause until others have had a chance to talk. Some are not as "fast on the draw" as others.

6. Do not worry about silence. People may be thinking. This is usually a good thing.

7. Try to listen to what the other person is really trying to say. See if you can rephrase accurately what was said. Test your perceptions occasionally by repeating what you thought the person said and ask if that is correct. If you do not understand a word or an idea or a suggestion, say so. Ask the person to try explaining it again or to give an illustration.

8. If another person is having trouble making a point, perhaps you can help him or her to clarify it. If a person is trying to get a word in but is crowded out, help that person to get the floor. If someone is timid or hesitant to speak, give encouragement. But don't rush in to finish sentences for others. Be careful about saying to someone, "I know what you are thinking" or "I know what you are feeling." Such statements are considered "mind reading" the

other person, and we may offend others if we happen to be wrong in our "hunch" about what they think or feel. It is better to simply ask what they think or feel.

9. Differences can be creative. Controversy may be a stimulus to a deeper study and understanding of the problem. To insist on conformity or to close out discussion too quickly may block the process. Insistence on one way to believe, interpret, or understand almost anything blocks the search for full truth on any topic or problem. Such narrow conformity and rigidity of thought will serve to block or regress a small group or even a large organization from its optimal growth and development.

10. Speak the truth (as you see it) in love. Reject ideas or disagree, but do not reject persons.

Workshop 4

Conflict in Values

A *value* is a belief, attitude, conviction, activity, or feeling that satisfies the following seven criteria: "(1) having been freely chosen, (2) having been chosen from among alternatives, (3) having been chosen after due reflection, (4) having been prized and cherished, (5) having been publicly affirmed, (6) having been incorporated into actual behavior, and (7) having been repeated in one's life."[1]

One's personal values regarding groups, persons, decision making, task and maintenance functions, leadership styles, conflict, and how to cope with group resistance are components of how one will function within a small group.

When the value(s) of one person conflict with those of others in the group, there are some common ways members usually react. These include fighting, taking flight, denying, agreeing, or compromising.

Leader Assignment

Read chapters 3 and 4. Duplicate Form 5, entitled "Verbal Conflict Observer Form," for all observers in this workshop. If participants have not been in Workshop 2, you will want to duplicate Forms 2 and 3. Also, duplicate copies of Form 3, entitled "How I Perceived the Person," for each participant's background information.

Outline for Workshop of Conflict in Values (two hours)

Purpose:

To discover through practice ways a group usually reacts to a values conflict and to consider alternative ways to react if needed.

Step 1 (thirty minutes):

Select several persons (two or three, depending on the size of the group) to serve as observers. Ask the remaining members to hold a discussion about one of the following issues: (1) whether to include five hundred dollars in the budget for the staff's continuing education, (2) whether to cut the volunteer-training budget by a thousand dollars, or (3) whether all new members must promise to give three hours of time to our organization before they can be admitted as members. Ask the three observers to watch for verbal patterns of (1) *fight* (to argue verbally), (2) *flight* (to change subject verbally or to leave room physically or psychologically), (3) *denial* (to deny conflict is occurring), and (4) *agreement* (to agree momentarily so as to avoid a conflict or argument). Observers should take notes and record actual quotes where possible. The observers may use Form 5, "Verbal Conflict Observer Form."

The same format may be used for a voluntary organization by talking about their budget, their staffing levels, and their program priorities.

Step 2 (fifteen minutes):

The observers give feedback to the discussion group (five minutes per observer) on what they observed in terms of their assigned observation role as given above.

Step 3 (thirty minutes):

Group resumes its original discussion while integrating any learnings from the feedback just received in Step 2. A new subject can be picked if it seems more profitable or interesting.

Step 4 (fifteen minutes):

Again, the observers give feedback to the group. Special attention will be given to any changes in their ability to cope with differences when their conflict is in relation to their values (five minutes per observer).

Step 5 (twenty-five minutes):

The total group enters into a discussion to: (1) identify learnings about how values conflict within a group, (2) identify what they discovered about their personal coping patterns when there is conflict with their values, and (3) identify what each coping pattern accomplished in the group.

Ask each person to identify what each would do differently if faced with a similar situation.

Step 6 (five minutes):

The leader shares with the group some of the highlights of chapter 4.

Form 5

Verbal Conflict Observer Form

Instructions to Observer

As you use this form, please make a tally mark in the appropriate box next to one of the four categories you believe you have just observed in the group of persons you are assigned to watch. Please write in an example of any quote you can recall that illustrates what you observed in any category below.

	Record tally here:	Write sample of comment here:
Fight—to fight verbally, argue, disagree, or discount.		
Flight—to change subject verbally, to leave room physically, or to withdraw psychologically.		
Denial—to deny that any verbal conflict is occurring.		
Agreement/Compromise—to agree to almost anything, momentarily, so as to avoid a conflict or argument at the moment.		

Workshop 5

Resistance and How to Cope with It

Resistance within a group involves resisting the leadership, the issues under discussion, the decision about to be made, or another person or persons within the group who wants to change something. Symptoms of resistance may include apathy, boredom, indifference, anger, confusion, or stalling/blocking behaviors to delay action. Resistance can be scary to deal with since few of us are experienced in dealing with it directly. Resistance can delay or regress a group when it is not dealt with directly and the resistance is permitted to run its course. If never dealt with, resistance can be destructive to a group or organization.

First, it is important to recognize that resistance is a symptom and not a cause. It is really a message to the group and its leadership that something else is going on but not being dealt with. Common causes of resistance are fear of change, lack of ownership in a decision, and fear of losing one's power or position of influence in the group. If the message is listened to, the group life will be maintained *by openly switching from a task to a maintenance function level immediately.* Then, when the real problem has been handled, the group can move on to the task level again.

Second, beginning to talk about the group resistance is the best way to begin coping with it. For example, persons who are invariably late to a group meeting or leave early from a group are resisters. Their lack of presence does influence, often negatively, the group process in reaching the group goal.

Third, resistance is often denied. Consequently, it is important to focus on the behavior evidenced rather than only on persons per se. For example, there have to be reasons why the whole group or a portion acts bored!

Fourth, resistance can be openly confronted if it is approached in terms of how we *appear* to be using our energy and how we feel about it. Ask: "Are there alternatives to what has been happening for us to consider?" "Is there a new way to behave that would be more productive and effective for us as a group?"

Leader Assignment

Read chapters 3 and 4 and 2 in that order. Duplicate copies of Form 6, entitled "Observer Form on Group Resistance," for use by the observers.

Outline for Workshop on Resistance and How to Cope with It (two hours)

Purpose:

To discover through practice the causes of resistance and what resistance can mean to a group and to consider new ways with which to cope with it.

Step 1 (thirty minutes):

The group will participate in a role-play. The situation for the role-play is a meeting of the membership committee of a church or voluntary organization. The chairperson has called the meeting to consider some plan to try to enlist into active participation in the life of the organization a group of members who have become inactive in attendance. Some of these people still give money and pay dues, while others are not contributing. The purpose of the group in the role-play is to develop a plan that will reenlist these people into active membership.

The leader will prepare small pieces of paper so that each member of the group will receive one. One piece of paper will say, "You are the chairperson"; three pieces of paper will say, "You are an observer"; half of the remaining papers will say, "You are to be positive and enthusiastic about the organization and the people who are not attending"; and the other half will say, "You are to be very negative about both the organization and the people who are not attending."

The observers are to use Form 6 as a guide in their observation. They will report in Step 2.

When the role-play is to begin, the leader sets the scene by reading the situation given above. When the role-play is finished, have the various role-players tell how they are feeling right now.

Step 2 (fifteen minutes):

The three observers will then give feedback to the group on their observations (five minutes per observer).

Step 3 (thirty minutes):

The group will continue its role-play. This time the enthusiasts will try to cope openly with the resistance of the apathetic resisting persons.

Step 4 (twenty-five minutes):

The members each tell how they are feeling right now. The observers again give feedback to the group indicating any differences in coping with resistance that they noted.

Step 5 (fifteen minutes):

In the total group, individuals will identify learnings about group resistance and how to cope with it. It is important to discuss feelings of all concerned and what might have been done differently in order to cope with resistance more effectively.

Step 6 (five minutes):

The leader shares with the group the information about resistance in groups found at the beginning of this workshop.

Form 6

Observer Form on Group Resistance

Instructions to Observer

As you use this form, please make a tally mark in the appropriate box next to one of the three categories you believe you have just observed (heard/seen) in the group of persons you are assigned to watch. Please write in an example of any quote you can recall that illustrates what you observed in any category.

	Record tally here:	Write sample comments here:
Verbal Resistance—lack of group discussion, including prolonged silences which feel uncomfortable; changing the subject; apathy; disinterest; challenging types of questions which cause confusion or group uneasiness.		
Nonverbal resistance—arms crossed, bored expressions, depressed expressions, leaving early or arriving late, permitting numerous phone interruptions, shuffling of feet, tapping of fingers on table.		
Coping with resistance—persons who **ask** questions about verbal or nonverbal forms of resistance, **suggest** group discuss when it feels resistance is occurring, make **suggestions** regarding an improvement in group norms, **confront** specific persons regarding their apparent resistance, give **feedback** to resisters if they request it.		

Workshop 6

Creative Conflict-Resolution Techniques

Interpersonal Conflict

The resolution of interpersonal conflict between two persons, and occasionally more than two persons, is one of the most dreaded scenarios in our culture. Most people try to avoid a confrontation, which is typical in two-person conflicts. Because of the hesitation most of us have in dealing directly with others with whom we have strong differences (conflicts), we naturally shy away from dealing with them directly if we can possibly avoid it. We can deny, avoid, procrastinate, get another to do it for us, or delay it in some fashion. When our feelings are very strong, our values are usually involved or threatened.

Leader Assignment

Read chapter 4 on the creative use of conflict. Next, consider whether it would be useful to use the process outline in the "Resources" section of this book entitled "Meetings for Two Persons." It is a brief process structured for the resolution of minor or minimal differences. It can be helpful in opening up the process between two persons prior to their willingness to proceed on to more major conflict issues between them.

Additional reading in the resource section can include the following pages: (1) principles of conflict utilization, (2) conflict utilization guide, and the (3) conflict intervention cycle. Additional reading may include the pages on (1) symptoms of distrust, (2) feedback, and (3) all three pages on various types of question framing techniques.

Outline for Workshop on Creative Conflict Resolution

Purpose:

To practice a method and set of skills in attempting to resolve an interpersonal conflict in as creative a manner as possible and with the least amount of emotionality.

Step 1 (fifteen to twenty minutes):

Ask for two volunteers to role-play a conflict situation wherein the two have a major difference about who will get 60 percent of their organization's budget for next year and who will receive the remaining 40 percent. They have been arguing about it for months. They have done their best to set political forces in motion to take their side against the other. Both clearly want their own way and are not interested in losing to the other. What can be done?

Ask two persons to volunteer to be informal "coaches" for person A and two more persons to volunteer to be "coaches" for person B. Ask the remaining persons in the workshop to volunteer to be observer teams in the following areas: (1) verbal patterns of persons A and B in the role-play; (2) nonverbal behaviors of persons A and B that may influence the outcome of the situation; (3) whether persons A and B stick to the agreed-on topic and agenda or whether they go off on other tangents or topics as a diversion; (4) whether or not the role-players are willing to negotiate or compromise for the larger good of the organization; and (5) whether or not persons A and B "personalize" issues that may be "impersonal." Each team will be asked to select a "reporter" to share its findings at the end of the workshop.

After people have volunteered and the leader has clarified the instructions for all concerned, including all observers and coaches, then the role-play may begin. It is important to instruct the "coaches" to talk with their assigned person A or B when the leader stops the role-players during the role-play. At those times the coaches talk with their person about how they are doing, whether they understand the process of what is happening, and whether they wish to consider any other type of response beyond what they have just said or done. Coaches can ask whether the person really wants to find a solution to the conflict or just defend his or her position. Does the person want to find out where the other person is *really* coming from and why he or she is taking the position so strongly. Does the person want to risk some form of collaboration or compromise with the other person and attempt to find a win-win solution as opposed to a win-lose solution?

Step 2 (seven to ten minutes):

The leader starts the role-play with persons A and B talking about their "conflict" described above. All observer teams observe according to their assigned topic. Observers are asked to take notes if they desire. After about seven to ten minutes the leader breaks in and stops the two role-players midstream and asks them to move their chairs back and talk quietly with their assigned "coaches."

Step 3 (five minutes):

The two role-players talk quietly with their respective coaches and essentially have a "time out" to reflect on the process of what has been happening.

Then, with any suggestions or ideas in mind from their coaches, the role-players move their chairs back and face each other again to resume the role-play while thinking about any changes or modifications they wish to incorporate into their approach to one another.

Step 4 (seven minutes):

The leader asks the two role-players to resume but to feel free to make any modifications in their statements or approach to one another that they may have received from their coaches during their time out. They resume and the leader again interrupts them mid-· stream in approximately seven minutes. Again, they are asked to move their chairs and talk quietly with their coaches.

Step 5 (five minutes):

During this five minutes the coaches can again make suggestions or just ask questions about what is happening and what is not happening. Then the role-player has time to think about what is happening in the process of trying to resolve a conflict with another person. Once again, they are asked to move their chairs back and resume the role-play. This time, the leader asks the role-players to see if they can demonstrate, with integrity, some type of approach that may (or may not) permit some form of conflict resolution of the alleged budget issue.

Step 6 (ten to twelve minutes):

The two role-players resume their alleged conflict but attempt some form of conflict resolution that demonstrates more of a win-win approach to the problem. Their approach will show concern for the overall good of the total organization as opposed to their smaller area of concern as a staff person. After a maximum of twelve minutes, the leader asks them to take a minute or so to conclude the role-play, whether they are completely done or not. The goal is to demonstrate understanding of process, learning from feedback from a personal coach, and trying on new skills and approaches for the first time in a conflict situation. Most of us never get an opportunity in which it is "safe" to practice and develop such skills and understandings when emotions run deep.

Step 7 (ten minutes):

Each role-player is asked to take a maximum of five minutes to share with the group his or her feelings, thoughts, insights, or questions about the role-play experience. The leader then checks with each role-player to clarify that they realize the role-play is over and that they are now done with that role and title. They are now back to being themselves and are to participate with their real names and not a role-player name. This is called "debriefing" and is important to always do when someone has been in a role-play.

Step 8 (thirty-five minutes):

Each coaching team is asked by the leader to give a maximum five-minute report on their observations of their role-player and what was happening. After each coaching team has reported out, each of the five observer team reporters is asked to give a maximum five-minute report on what their team observed in the total role-play of persons A and B and what happened.

Step 9 (fifteen to twenty minutes):

The leader then opens up the discussion for all to discuss the role-play, what they saw happening, what they learned about conflict resolution skills and approaches, and what they would do differently if they had been involved in it. The leader makes a summary statement for the overall workshop and adjourns the group.

Summary of Workshop

Methods/Skills for Creative Conflict Utilization

1. State the problem/issue in terms of cooperation rather than competition.

2. Agree to deal with one issue at a time.

3. Avoid taking things too personally.

4. Work toward a win-win type solution rather than a win-lose solution.

5. Agree to take "time outs" and have brief conferences or consultations with others and then return to the resolution process.

6. We often predetermine the outcome of a conflict scenario with a silent decision to resolve or block the resolution somehow. If we decide to resolve it, we have a better opportunity to do so since we convey that "attitude" as we begin our approach to the other person.

7. Talk about what you actually know and understand. Ask for clarification and additional information for areas you do not understand.

8. Set time limits before beginning so that discussions do not continue unduly long.

9. Ask about where the other person is coming from and what he or she knows and understands. What does that person believe may be rumor or distortion? How does the other person define the problem or issue? What is his or her perspective? What are his or her assumptions?

10. Consider creating a third (or neutral) option that may be a combination of what each of you desires in order to gain resolution. Can both parties agree to this third option that they have helped create?

Resources

Person Awareness and Communication

Guidelines for Question Framing:

Don't
—Ask "yes" and "no" questions.
—Ask probing questions.
—Ask judgmental (evaluating) questions.
—Ask questions that imply an answer or a point of view.
—Ask questions that reveal your own prejudice.

Do
—Ask questions to surface more facts.
—Ask questions that reduce threat.
—Ask questions that support the person while encouraging objectivity.
—Ask questions that focus on reality.
—Ask questions that encourage the person to continue talking.

Four Factors in Empathetic Listening:

1. Hear the other's words (content).
2. Hear the other's point of view (attitude).
3. Hear the other's feelings.
4. Maintain your objectivity (get your point of view out of the way).

For Empathetic Communication:

—Understand your own feelings.
—Get in touch with the other's feelings.
—Frame questions that release and free the other.
—Exercise empathetic listening.
—Use participant-observation skills.

The Questioning Techniques

Direction of Questions

Type	Purpose	Examples
A. Overhead Directed to group.	1. To open discussion.	1. How shall we begin?
	2. To introduce new phase.	2. What should we consider next, anyone?
	3. To give everyone a chance to comment.	3. What else might be important?
B. Direct Addressed to a specific person.	1. To call on person for specific information.	1. Al, what would be your suggestions?
	2. To involve someone who has not been active.	2. Fred, have you had any experience with this?
C. Relay Referred back to another person or to the group.	1. To help leader avoid giving own opinion.	1. Would someone like to comment on Judy's question?
	2. To get others involved in the discussion.	2. Jane, how would you answer Judy's question?
	3. To call on someone who knows the answer.	
D. Reverse Referred back to the person who asked question.	1. To help leader avoid giving own opinion.	1. Well, Dick, how about giving us your opinion first?
	2. To encourage questioner to think for himself or herself.	2. Jean, tell us first what you own experience has been.
	3. To bring out opinions.	

Guidelines for Framing Questions

Do's and Don'ts

The following is a list of do's and don'ts on framing questions with explanation:

Do

—Focus questions on data.* What are the situations in your class that are causing difficulty?

—Ask questions that allow the interviewee to become involved. Who are the people in your class or group? Tell me about them.

—Help the interviewee see that you don't know the answer. What are the ways in which we can explore this problem?

—Ask questions so that they are free to answer on their level. Where do you find your hardest binds in your role as teachers or leaders?

—Ask reality-testing questions. What occurred in your class or group when you tried it that way?

Don't

—Ask questions to which a concrete answer cannot be given. What do you suppose the people are thinking about when they come to your class or group?

—Ask questions that can be answered "yes" or "no". Do you have problems as a teacher or leader?

—Attempt to lead the interviewee to your answer or the one you expect. Don't you really need to improve your own session planning?

—Ask threatening or motivational questions. Why do you feel that way?

—Ask questions that lead to vague intellectualizing. What is the best approach to teaching the subject or leading the group?

---

*There are many kinds of data to be aware of, such as feeling tones, conceptual understanding, behavioral skill, group process, future expectations.

Framing Questions

Type	Purpose	Examples
1. **Factual**	To get information	All the "W" questions
	To open discussion	What? Where? Why? When? Who? and How?
2. **Explanatory**	To get reasons and explanations	In what way would this help solve the problem?
	To broaden discussion	What other aspects of this should be considered?
	To develop additional information	Just how would this be done?
3. **Justifying**	To challenge old ideas	Why do you think so?
	To develop new ideas	How do you know?
	To get reasoning and proof	What evidence do you have?
4. **Leading**	To introduce new ideas	Should we consider this a possible solution?
	To advance a suggestion of of your own or others	Would this—be a feasible alternative?
5. **Hypothetical**	To develop new ideas	Suppose we did it this way—
	To suggest another, possibly unpopular opinion	What would happen? Another group does— Is this feasible here?
6. **Alternative**	To make decision between alternatives	Which of these solutions is the best? —A or —B? Or A and B combined?
	To get agreement	Does this represent our choice in preference to —?
7. **Coordinating**	To develop consensus	Can we conclude that this is the next step?
	To get agreement	
	To take action	Is there general agreement then on this plan?

The Team Helpers

The Helping Process

The *goal* of the helping process is to produce constructive *change* in the receiver of help: to clarify the receiver's perception of the problem, to bolster the receiver's self-confidence, to modify the receiver's behavior (or develop new skills). The receiver of change alone determines whether or not change takes place.

Difficulties in Receiving Help	Difficulties in Giving Help
1. Hard to admit difficulties to self.	1. Need to demonstrate competence (feel that we ought to be able to give "good" advice).
2. Hard to admit difficulties to others.	2. Need to win. Therefore, respond with increased pressure (arguing) to the other's resistance.
3. Work norms (such as competition) make it difficult to establish trust.	3. Needs for warmth—leads to oversupport. Needs for fight—leads to overcriticism.
4. Fear that we lower our esteem in the eyes of others.	
5. Dependency problems: *counterdependency*—committed to resisting all influence from others. *dependency*—more interested in relying on others than solving problem.	
6. Really looking for sympathy or support (not change).	
7. Helping process may lead to looking at a side of ourselves we'd like to avoid looking at.	

Experimental studies of the helping process indicate that change is most likely to occur when the receiver sees in the giver:

1. Unconditional regard—The receiver is accepted regardless of what he or she says or does.

2. Empathetic understanding—The giver communicates that he or she feels the situation the receiver describes.

3. Authenticity—The receiver feels that he or she and the giver can be open, honest, and free with each other.

—by Dr. Barry Oshry

Trust

One author offers this definition of trust.

When you self-disclose to another person you are engaging in trust when you

1. are aware that your choice to be open could lead to beneficial (a closer relationship) or harmful (rejection, ridicule) consequences;

2. realize that the consequences of your choice depend upon the behavior of the other person;

3. expect to suffer much more if your trust is violated (and you are rejected) than you would gain if your trust is fulfilled (and the relationship develops);

4. feel relatively confident that the other will behave in such a way that the beneficial consequences will result.

—from Reaching Out: InterPersonal Effectiveness and Self-Actualization by David W. Johnson[1]

Problem-solving groups with high trust will: (1) exchange relevant ideas and feelings more openly, (2) develop greater clarification of goals and problems, (3) search more extensively for alternative courses of action, (4) have greater influence on solutions, (5) be more satisfied with their problem-solving efforts, (6) have greater motivation to implement conclusions, (7) see themselves as closer and more of a team, and (8) have less desire to leave their group to join another.

—from Interpersonal Conflict Resolution by Alan C. Filley[2]

Symptoms of Distrust

The following list of the symptoms of distrust in individuals and in groups briefly describes what to look for in trying to determine the level of trust in yourself, another person, or a group. As trust and a climate of openness grow, these symptoms of distrust will subside:

—persistent defense of public image
—attempts to change attitudes or beliefs of others
—attempts to make decisions for others
—avoidance of feeling or exposure of feeling
—avoidance of conflict
—advice-giving
—flattery
—cynicism about the powers of another person or the group
—derogation of another person's or the group's abilities
—maintenance of formality in behavior or control mechanisms
—lack of confidence in the product of the group
—denial of membership
—insistence upon control
—rigid preplanning of group agenda
—preservation of social distance
—fear of controversy
—attempts to find strong or expert leaders
—insistence on formal rules
—insistence on keeping things on an impersonal basis
—assigning critical functions of problem solving and group
   maintenance to designated or implicitly appointed leaders

Principles of Conflict Utilization
by Nathan W. Turner

Conflict may be simply defined as a disagreement and/or difference over ideas, attitudes, values, feelings, or behavior between two or more persons. Many conflicts arise from misunderstandings between persons because of poor communication. Some conflicts arise because of no communication and lack of personal relationship. Broken contracts can also set off conflict(s).

A basic principle in conflicts is to utilize the energy involved in a productive manner. Conflict stirs up feelings in persons, and the issue is what happens to the feelings? Is the energy from these feelings held inside and bottled up? Is the energy allowed to escape in one huge burst or blast? Or, is the energy released gradually and channeled towards a goal of improved relationships between the persons involved? Therefore, energy in conflict ought to become something we value and utilize rather than avoid.

The following are principles of conflict utilization.

1. Value conflict(s). Use the energy rather than holding it in.

2. Confront small issues before they grow too big.

3. Focus on issues, situations, and real problems rather than attacking personality, family, and motives.

4. Suppressing and repressing conflict only serves to delay more serious conflict(s) later.

5. Settling differences over positives is easier than over negatives.

6. Acknowledge that many conflicts arise from a need or desire to control another or control a situation.

7. Clarify who "owns" the problem, who is affected by it, and why.

8. Clarify what has changed in the situation or relationship.

9. Clarify what is known to either person or both.

10. Clarify how each sees the situation, and how each feels about it.

11. Clarify what the situation is.

12. Obtain clear definition by all persons of what the real problem is.

13. Look for all possible alternatives or combinations of alternatives.

14. Accept that conflict is inevitable.

15. Realize that conflict is cyclical and predictable.

Conflict Intervention Cycle

© 1986, Nathan W. Turner

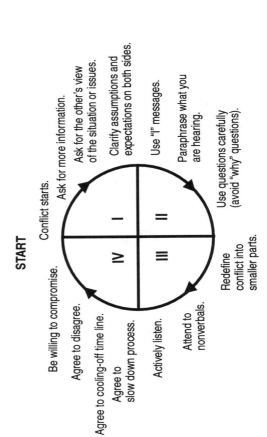

START

Conflict starts.

Ask for more information.

Ask for the other's view of the situation or issues.

Clarify assumptions and expectations on both sides.

Use "I" messages.

Paraphrase what you are hearing.

Use questions carefully (avoid "why" questions).

Redefine conflict into smaller parts.

Attend to nonverbals.

Actively listen.

Agree to slow down process.

Agree to cooling-off time line.

Agree to disagree.

Be willing to compromise.

I II III IV

Conflict Utilization Guide

Conflict is often confusing since it functions on many levels. A conflict can become worse due to various parties attempting to resolve it on different levels without realizing that they are approaching one another on different levels. The following guide is intended to clarify some of the possible levels. You are invited to check off the relevant boxes that are typical levels in which you may function during a conflict situation.

Level of Conflict	Description of the Level	Common Conflict Resolution Methods	Place a check mark if you tend to function on that level
I. Perceptions	Persons hold different perceptions of situations	Clarify issues; Clarify values held	
II. Goals or purposes	Different goals or purposes clash or have different values	Try to understand the other's goals/purposes; Assign priority status to each one and negotiate	
III. Processes	Conflict over whether facts or personal relationships should be dealt with	Redefine into a both/and approach and deal with both relationships and facts in that order	
IV. Methods		Redefine the conflict into a problem-solving approach rather than a personality attack or power struggle	
V. Personality differences	Personality conflict with another person—usually for "personal" reasons or feelings	Often third-party consultation and intervention will be necessary. Or agree to disagree.	
VI. Values	Values are the areas in which we hold our deepest feelings. Both meanings and perceptions may differ	Usually third-party intervention will be necessary to deal with such conflicts	

Checklist on Communications

Check yourself for identification of some of your "communications practices."

Personal Checklist

In my own communication I find myself:

	Most of the time	Some of the time	Need to improve
1. Saying what I really think rather than what is "acceptable."			
2. Checking what the other person has said before evaluating.			
3. Listening for the other person's point of view before replying.			
4. Making it possible for others to tell me differing ideas.			
5. Assuming that what is clear to me may not be clear to the receiver.			
6. Being influenced by a persuasive speaker because of his or her appearance, manner, and decibel strength.			
7. Thinking in stereotypes.			
8. Making up my mind on the basis of the first approach.			
9. Getting annoyed with others because they do not seem to understand what I am saying.			

Date _____

Feedback

Feedback is a way of helping others to consider changing their behavior. It is communication to a person (or group) that gives others information about how they affect someone else. As in a guided missile system, feedback helps individuals keep their behavior "on target" and thus better achieve their goals.

Some criteria for useful feedback:

1. It is descriptive rather than evaluative. By describing one's own reaction, it leaves the other individual free to use it or not to use it as he or she sees it. By avoiding evaluative language, it reduces the need for the individual to react defensively.

2. It is specific rather than general. To be told that one is "dominating" will probably not be as useful as to be told that "just now when we were deciding the issue, you did not listen to what others said, and I felt forced to accept your arguments or face attack from you."

3. It takes into account the needs of both the receiver and giver of feedback. Feedback can be destructive when it serves only our own needs and fails to consider the needs of the person on the receiving end.

4. It is directed toward behavior that the receiver can do something about. Frustration is only increased when a person is reminded of some shortcoming over which he or she has no control.

5. It is best solicited rather than imposed. Feedback is most useful when the receiver himself or herself has formulated the kind of question that those observing him or her can answer.

6. It is well-timed. In general, feedback is most useful at the earliest opportunity after the given behavior occurs (depending, of course, on the person's readiness to hear it, support available from others, and so on).

7. It is *checked* to insure clear communication. One way of doing this is to have the receiver try to rephrase the feedback he or she has received to see if it corresponds to what the sender had in mind.

8. When feedback is given in a training group, both giver and receiver have opportunity to check with others in the group the

accuracy of the feedback. Is this one person's impression or an impression shared by others?

Feedback is not a subtle way of forcing another to reveal himself or herself. Feedback, then, is a way of giving help; it is a corrective mechanism for individuals who want to learn how well their behavior matches their intentions; and it is a means for establishing one's identity, for answering, "Who am I?"

Meetings for Two Persons

Purposes

1. To share disappointments, frustrations, desired changes, and the like with one another

2. To specify what each expects of the other (now)

3. To clarify how each one's expectations are not being satisfied

4. To negotiate changes both in the area of expectations and in the manner (style) of how the expectations are met

5. To increase the helpfulness aspect of their relationship

Method

1. Each person writes three lists (alone):

a. Positive feedback list: things the person values in the way the two have worked together and/or related

b. "Bug" list: things the person has not liked or cannot tolerate

c. Empathy list: a prediction of what the other person has on his or her lists

2. Each person presents his or her positive feedback and "bug" lists to the other; then they share their empathy lists. During this time, the third-party consultant discourages any talk not directed specifically toward gaining an understanding of the other's point of view.

3. Each person then offers any information and/or views that may clarify matters. Again, general discussion is barred.

4. Next, each person begins to negotiate changes he or she wants. They mutually consent to planned changes and then decide upon how they will work together (as a two-person team) to bring them about. The third-party consultant lists the agreed-upon actions to

be taken by both persons. The consultant also lists those issues still unresolved and needing future meetings to resolve.

The two persons then decide how these unresolved issues will be dealt with, or perhaps agree that they will remain unresolved for a specific period of time with the proviso that both will "live with" the issues still unresolved.

5. The two persons plan all necessary follow-up steps including the setting of dates, locations, and responsibilities.

Adapted by Nathan W. Turner and Associates (10/83)
from Jack R. Fordyce and Raymond Weil, Managing with People:
A Manager's Handbook of Organization Development Methods
(Reading, Mass.: Addison-Wesley Publishing Co., 1971), 114-115.

Increasing Your Capacity to Cope with Stress

You can increase your capacity to cope with stress in three ways:
1. *Reduce* the quantity and/or difficulty of the tasks that confront you.
2. *Reduce* the time pressure you are under to complete the tasks.
3. *Increase* your coping skills through reeducation.

—Sidney Lecker, The Natural Way to Stress Control (New York: Grosset and
Dunlap Publishers, 1978) [3]

The Relaxation Response[4]

by Herbert Benson

Background: The fight-or-flight response prepares a person for fighting or fleeing because of increased adrenaline in the bloodstream. The relaxation response is an opposite response in which there is a general quieting in the body when the relaxation response takes effect. There is also decreased blood pressure and marked decrease in metabolism.

When and Where: A person should bring about the response during a busy working day by slowing down the business pace for ten to twenty minutes two or three times a day. During this period, a person combating tension should sit quietly, contemplating or meditating. Incoming telephone calls should be diverted, and all other distractions should be set aside.

The Four Steps

1. Select a quiet place. A quiet office will do nicely. An airliner is another good place for a business person to relax in; a modern jet is not too noisy, and the traveler has time to spare. Sit upright, but be comfortable.

2. Select a word or phrase, or compose a short prayer. The word, phrase, or prayer should be repeated over and over—not aloud, but to yourself.

3. Adopt a passive attitude. Let things happen. Don't combat anything. Just repeat the word, phrase, or prayer time and again.

4. Close your eyes, but do not go to sleep.

Results: The relaxation response should be built into your life and should become part of your lifestyle. The bottom line for all this is relaxation, less illness, decreased blood pressure, better job satisfaction, and improved work.

Planning Steps for Action

1. Clearly identify the problem to be solved or the goal to be achieved. Is it real? Do I care? Can I make a real difference in the situation?

2. Identify the forces working for and against the solution to the problem or the achievement of the goal. Include persons, events, forces, and so on.

3. Review the positive and negative forces at work, and choose the factors that are the most important to you at this moment. What restraining force really "bugs you" or holds you back? What driving forces can you really depend on?

4. For each restraining force, list as many action steps as you can. Brainstorm. Select one or two you'd really like to work on.

5. For each driving force, list as many action steps as you can that will work for you. Select one or two that will be a real resource to you.

6. Choose your point of beginning. That is a place where you have the most going for you and at the same time, your actions *will* *not* increase the restraining forces.

7. **For each action step, indicate the kinds of resources you will need.** Resources include persons, materials, events, and so forth.

8. **Figure out how you are going to evaluate your progress toward your goal once you begin to implement your action plan.** List the evaluation procedures you will use.

9. **Implement your action steps. Put your action plan to work for you.**

10. **Evaluate what you have done. Find out where your strengths and weaknesses are.** Revise and implement your plan of action.

Notes

Chapter 1

1. A group norm (or standard) means that group members tend to exhibit relative uniformity (similarity) in opinions and behaviors. That is, people are strongly influenced by the groups to which they belong.

2. Miriam A. Peterson, *The Role of Small Groups and Group Leadership in the Church's Ministry* (Valley Forge, Pa.: The Department of Ministry with Adults, American Baptist Board of Education and Publication, 1967).

3. Roger M. Schwarz, *The Skilled Facilitator: Practical Wisdom for Developing Effective Groups* (San Francisco: Jossey-Bass Inc., Publishers, 1994). Reprinted with permission.

4. Ibid., Figure 4.1, 68.

Chapter 2

1. Susan A. Wheelan, *Group Processes: A Developmental Perspective* (Boston: Allyn and Bacon, 1994).

2. Nathan W. Turner, "Conflict Utilization in Marital-Dyadic Therapy," *Psychiatric Clinics of North America,* vol. 5, no. 3, *December 1982, 503.*

3. Wheelan, 119.

4. William C. Schutz, *The Interpersonal Underworld* (Palo Alto, Calif.: Science and Behavior Books, Inc., 1966).

5. Ibid.

Chapter 3

1. Miriam A. Peterson, *The Role of Small Groups and Group Leadership in the Church's Ministry* (Valley Forge, Pa.: The Department of Ministry with Adults, American Baptist Board of Education and Publication, 1967).

2. David W. Johnson and Frank P. Johnson, *Joining Together: Group Theory and Group Skills* (Boston: Allyn and Bacon, 1975). Reprinted and adapted by permission.

3. Robert F. Bales, "A Set of Categories for the Analysis of Small Group Interaction," *American Sociological Review,* vol. 15 (1950), 257-263, as cited in Theodore M. Mills, *The Sociology of Small Groups* (Englewood Cliffs, N.J.: Prentice-Hall, Inc., 1967), 31. Reprinted by permission of the University of Chicago Press.

4. Developed by Nathan W. Turner, adapted from Bales, "Categories."

5. Reprinted with permission of the National Training Laboratories, National Education Association, from the Notebook of the Third Protestant Laboratory on Group Development and Leadership.

6. Peterson, Ibid.

7. Daniel, Sankowsky, "The Charismatic Leader as Narcissist: Understanding the Abuse of Power," *Organizational Dynamics,* Spring 1995, Exhibit 2, 67.

Chapter 4

1. Nathan W. Turner, "Conflict Utilization in Marital-Dyadic Therapy," *Psychiatric Clinics of North America,* vol. 5, no. 3, December 1982, 504.

2. Adapted with permission of the National Training Laboratories, National Education Association, from the Notebook of the Third Protestant Laboratory on Group Development and Leadership.

3. Ibid.

Chapter 5

1. Reprinted and adapted with the permission of The Free Press,

a division of Simon & Shuster from *DECISION MAKING: A Psychological Analysis of Conflict, Choice, and Commitment* by Irving L. Janis and Leon Mann. Copyright 1977.

2. Ibid., 129-133.

3. Ibid., 132.

4. Ibid., 172.

5. Ibid., 407.

6. Ibid., 52-80.

7. R. L. Veninga and J. P. Spradley, *The Work Stress Connection: How to Cope With Job Burnout* (New York: Ballantine Books, 1981).

8. Sidney Lecker, *The Natural Way to Stress Control* (New York: Grosset & Dunlap Publishers, 1978).

9. Herbert Benson, *The Relaxation Response* (New York: Morrow, 1975).

Chapter 6

1. R. M. Kanter, *The Change Masters: Innovation for Productivity in the American Corporation* (New York: Simon & Schuster, 1983), 279, 32.

2. Ibid., 28.

3. E. H. Schein, *Organizational Culture and Leadership* (San Francisco, Calif.: Jossey-Bass Publishers, 1985), 14-20.

4. P. M. Senge, *The Fifth Discipline: The Art & Practice of the Learning Organization* (New York: Doubleday/Currency, 1990), 68, 73.

5. Ibid., 79-84.

6. Ibid., 345.

Chapter 7

1. L.E. Raths, M. Harmin, and S.B. Simon, *Values and Teaching: Working with Values in the Classroom* (Columbus, Ohio: Charles E. Merrill Publishing Company, 1966), 46.

Resources

1. David W. Johnson, *Reaching Out: Interpersonal Effectiveness*

and Self-Actualization (Englewood Cliffs, N.J.: Prentice-Hall, Inc. 1972), 45.

2. Alan C. Filley, *Interpersonal Conflict Resolution* (Glenview, Ill.: Scott, Foresman and Co., 1975), 68.

3. Sidney Lecker, *The Natural Way to Stress Control* (New York: Grosset & Dunlap Publishers, 1978).

4. Herbert Benson, *The Relaxation Response* (New York: Morrow, 1975).

Bibliography

Bennis, Warren, and Nanus, Burt. *The Strategies for Taking Charge.* New York: Harper & Row Publishers, 1985.

Benson, Herbert. *The Relaxation Response.* New York: Morrow, 1975.

Cartwright, Darwin, and Zander, Alvin, eds. *Group Dynamics: Research and Theory,* 3d ed. New York: Harper & Row, Publishers, 1968.

Covey, Stephen R. *The Seven Habits of Highly Effective People*: *Restoring the Character of Ethic.* New York: Simon & Schuster, 1990.

Deutsch, Morton. "Conflicts: Productive and Destructive." *Journal of Social Issues.* Vol. 25, 1969.

Filley, Alan C. *Interpersonal Conflict Resolution,* Glenview, Ill.: Scott, Foresman & Co., 1975.

Fordyce, Jack, K and Weil, Raymond. *Managing with People: A Manager's Handbook of Organization Methods.* (Reading, Mass.: Addison-Wesley Publishing Co., 1971.

Halverstadt, Hugh F. *Managing Church Conflict.* Louisville: Westminster/John Knox Press, 1991.

Janis, Irving L. and Mann, Leon. *Decision Making, A Psychological Analysis of Conflict, Choice, and Commitment.* New York: The Free Press, 1977.

Johnson, David W., and Johnson, Frank P. *Joining Together: Group*

Theory and Group Skills. Englewood Cliffs, N.J.: Prentice Hall, Inc., 1975.

Johnson, David W. *Reaching Out: Interpersonal Effectiveness and Self Actualization.* Englewood Cliffs, N.J.: Prentice-Hall, Inc., 1972.

Kanter, Rosabeth Moss. *The Change Masters: Innovation for Productivity in the American Corporation.* New York: Simon & Schuster, 1983.

Leas, Speed. Moving Your Church Through Conflict. Bethesda, Md.: An Alban Institute Publication, 1985.

Leas, Speed, and Kittlaus, Paul. *Church Fights: Managing Conflict in the Local Church.* Philadelphia: The Westminister Press, 1973.

Lecker, Sidney. *The Natural Way to Stress Control.* New York: Grosset & Dunlap Publishers, 1978.

Lewin, Kurt. *Resolving Social Conflicts.* New York: Harper & Row, Publishers, 1948.

Leypoldt, Martha M. *Learning Is Change.* Valley Forge, Pa.: Judson Press, 1971.

_____. *40 Ways to Teach in Groups.* Rev. ed. Valley Forge, Pa.: Judson Press, 1992.

Luft, Joseph. *Group Processes: An Introduction to Group Dynamics,* Rev. ed. Palo Alto, Calif.: National Press Books, 1970.

Marshall, Edward M. *Transforming the Way We Work: The Power of the Collaborative Workplace.* New York: American Management Association, 1995.

McGregor, Douglas. *The Human Side of Enterprise.* New York: McGraw Hill Book & Education Services Group, 1960.

Peterson, Miriam A. *The Role of Small Groups and Group Leadership in the Church's Ministry.* Valley Forge, Pa.: Department of Adult Ministry, American Baptist Churches of the United States of America, 1968.

Raths, Louis E., Harmin, Merrill, and Simon, Sidney B. *Values and Teaching: Working with Values in the Classroom.* Columbus,

Ohio: Charles E. Merrill Publishing Company, 1966.

Schein, Edgar H. *Organizational Culture and Leadership.* San Francisco, Calif.: Jossey-Bass Publishers, 1985.

Schutz, William C. *The Interpersonal Underworld.* Palo Alto, Calif.: Science and Behavior Books, Inc., 1966.

Schutz, William C. *Joy: Expanding Human Awareness.* New York: Grove Press, Inc., 1968.

Schwarz, Roger M. *The Skilled Facilitator: Practical Wisdom for Developing Effective Groups.* San Francisco, Calif.: Jossey-Bass Publishers, 1994.

Selye, Hans. *Stress Without Distress.* New York: Signet Books, 1974.

Senge, Peter M. *The Fifth Discipline: The Art & Practice of the Learning Organization.* New York: Doubleday/Currency, 1990.

Turner, Nathan, W. "Conflict Utilization in Marital-Dyadic Therapy." *Psychiatric Clinics of North America.* Vol. 5, No. 3. December 1982.

Veninga, Robert L., and Spradley, James P. *The Work Stress Connection: How to Cope With Job Burnout.* New York: Ballantine Books, 1981.

Watson, Goodwin, and Johnson, David W. *Social Psychology: Issues and Insights.* Philadelphia: J. B. Lippincott Company, 1972.

Wheelan, Susan A. *Group Processes: A Developmental Perspective.* Boston: Allyn and Bacon, 1994.